In a Dark Time

In a Dark Time

A Prisoner's Struggle for Healing and Change

Dwight Harrison and Susannah Sheffer

Stone Lion Press
Amherst, Massachusetts

For information about discounts on bulk orders for classrooms, groups, and organizations, please visit our website at www.stonelionpress.com.

Grateful acknowledgment is made for permission to reprint the following material:
Excerpt from "In a Dark Time," copyright (c) 1960 by Beatrice Roethke, Administratrix of the Estate of Theodore Roethke, from *Complete Poems of Theodore Roethke* by Theodore Roethke. Used by permission of Doubleday, a division of Random House, Inc.

This is a work of non-fiction. Some names and identifying details have been changed to protect the privacy of individuals mentioned in the text.

Publisher's Cataloging-In-Publication Data
(Prepared by The Donohue Group, Inc.)

Harrison, Dwight D. 1957-
    In a dark time : a prisoner's struggle for healing and change / Dwight Harrison and Susannah Sheffer.

    p. ; cm.
    ISBN: 0-9764309-0-8 (alk. paper)

1. Prisoners--Massachusetts--Personal narratives. 2. Men--Imprisonment--Massachusetts--20th century. 3. Criminals--Rehabilitation--Massachusetts--20th century. I. Sheffer, Susannah. II. Title.

HV6089 .H37 2005
365.44   2004117330

Cover design: Angela Mark
Interior design: Patrick Farenga

Printed and bound in the United States of America
10 9 8 7 6 5 4 3 2 1

In a dark time, the eye begins to see. ...

I know the purity of pure despair,
My shadow pinned against a sweating wall.
That place among the rocks – is it a cave
Or winding path? The edge is what I have. ...

Dark, dark my light, and darker my desire.
My soul, like some heat-maddened summer fly,
Keeps buzzing at the sill. Which I is *I*?
A fallen man, I climb out of my fear.
The mind enters itself, and God the mind,
And one is One, free in the tearing wind.

– from "In a Dark Time," by Theodore Roethke

One week out of prison, walking as a free man for the first time in almost seventeen years, I enter the Registry of Motor Vehicles expecting the worst. In my pocket I've got two pieces of identifying information, not the three they require. Everyone has warned me about the hassle this will be.

Waiting in line, I start talking to the man behind me. He says he's a defense attorney, of all things.

"I just got out of prison," I tell him, the way I've been telling it to everyone – so I can say it first, before they find it out or guess. "I'm trying to get my Massachusetts State I.D. here, but I know I'm gonna have trouble."

"Hey, everything will be all right," he says. Where has *he* been? And who believes a lawyer's promises?

I reach the head of the line and as soon as I start trying to explain myself to the woman behind the desk, she says I'll have to see a supervisor. *Here we go,* I think to myself as I walk down the hall to the supervisor's office. *Now the trouble starts.* I start bracing myself for it. I won't beg them.

"This is my situation," I begin telling the supervisor. "I just got out of prison last week. I did nearly seventeen years, and I don't have any I.D., just my birth certificate and a letter saying where I'm living. I don't want to be walking around without any I.D., because I don't feel like I belong out here as it is, and I don't need the police hassling me –"

She takes my letter and the birth certificate and says, "Follow me." I follow her to her office, where she does something I can't see. We go back to the original desk, and she says to the first woman, "It's OK; I've approved this." She turns to go and I'm standing there trying to take it in when I hear her voice again. "Dwight," she says, and I startle because it's been years since I've heard my first name from anyone in charge. I look up to see what she wants, and she says, "Welcome back."

There it was, compassion so simple it could almost seem ordinary.

But it practically brought me to tears in the registry hallway. In that moment I began to feel that maybe I really was back, back from prison's brutal desert, back from the exile of my own pain and rage.

Returned to the world, released straight from a medium security prison to the street, and any preparation I had I'd gotten myself. There was no pre-release program, nothing set up to help me think the process through. After sixteen years and eight months, there was just a day that finally came.

"At least you've got a date," lifers would say to the rest of us when we complained about how much time we had left to do. It's true, we had official release dates, calculated the moment we arrived and continually readjusted according to the "good time" we earned or lost. But when I came to prison at age 21, that release date seemed as far off as never. I couldn't imagine living long enough to do a 28-30-year sentence, even if the law said you wrapped a sentence after serving two-thirds of it and were eligible for parole in even less time. I couldn't imagine living long enough to become the kind of man anyone *would* welcome back.

This is what exile looks like: its walls are beige, its doors are solid steel and locked. When the keepers snap the cuffs on you or slip your tray through the slot or tell you to bend over for the search, the knowledge is everywhere in their posture, in their faces: *we can do anything to you. There are no eyes here but ours.*

And this is also what exile looks like: a boy coming home one night and realizing he is invisible. No one sees what happens to him, no one stands in the space where he is standing. The doors here are not steel, not visible, but they are, somehow, unopenable. There is no way to get from where he is to where all the other people are. And so the knowledge is everywhere in his posture, in his face: anything can happen. I can do anything to anybody, because it doesn't matter. I am not where they are. I am not who they are.

I never expected to be welcomed back. I never expected mercy in that registry supervisor's eyes, I never expected it from the prison guards, and by the time I landed in prison I had given up expecting to find mercy in the faces of anyone who was supposed to be older and wiser. Sometimes now I think about how mercy feels – that surprise relenting, that softening – and I think about how there was no mercy in my own eyes twenty years ago. Not for my victims, not for myself.

If mercilessness was the wall between me and the rest of the world, what I have now are doors, possibilities of entry, so that I can let other people in and be let in by them, be welcomed back. And even if looking into my own eyes is still the hardest thing of all, at least the coldness is gone. Without that coldness I am not the man who went into prison. It means that during those years some change happened, a thaw that was both agonizing and healing. It didn't happen all at once and it didn't always happen in a way that you could readily see, but it did happen.

It did happen, and I did return. *Welcome back*, the registry supervisor said. If exile is all about solitude, return has to be about other people. It's about being brought back, *letting* oneself be brought back, figuring out how to be drawn back into the circle. And that too doesn't happen all at once. But I can say that where I am now is here, feet firmly planted in the soil of my new life, and I can say too that I carry the years of exile inside me, holes that I have to bear and can never entirely fill because the scars won't let me. But that's what freedom is, or so I sometimes think – accepting the limitations that are not in the bars and the walls but in the limits of your own skin, your own life story. Accepting it, and then not giving up, but still trying every day to come more of the way back.

Part of coming back must be about understanding how you went so far away. Understanding how it happened. Sitting in a coffee shop a year after walking out the prison door, I'm looking out the window at the people hurrying home from work, calling to each other across the street, disappearing down the steps of the subway. Most days, I'm actually starting to take all this for granted, but today for some reason I notice everything. Maybe because June in Boston always makes me watchful. The June day that brought me here nearly 18 years ago is never far from my mind. Or maybe I know that there is really nothing ordinary about sitting here like this. Nothing ordinary about any kind of second chance. I walked in like any man, asked for coffee, handed over a couple of dollars and got my change. The guy at the register didn't say *what the hell are you doing here*, so maybe my years of exile don't show.

I take a drink of coffee and look down at my hands. If I could just live inside this moment and nowhere else, there might be peace in it. But these hands! Today they might only be holding this cup, scratching my dog's ears or rubbing the cat's stomach until he purrs. But what they've done in the past – there's no escaping it. I have to find a way to live with what they've done. What I've done.

Some say I've already done my reckoning, accounted for what needs accounting. That's what it means to agree to everything the judge asks you. That's what it means to serve out your prison sentence. But saying those words, even serving the time, is no guarantee of anything. Armed robbery and attempted murder are the charges on record. I need to show what those words meant to me and to three other people on one particular June day. And I need to go back even farther and try to figure out how I came to be the man standing in that place on that day. Looking out this window, I know that if I want to join the world really, all the way, I need to tell this story through.

If you fling something away, what does it take to get it back? When I was six and skipping oyster shells across the swamp, the flinging was exuberant. I caught tadpoles and held them in my cupped hands and then let them go, no regrets, just an easy hold and release. And my dog Sparky, a frenzied mix of basset hound and beagle, chased every stick I threw for him and brought it back as if retrieval was always that sure.

We lived on Greenway Avenue in Winston-Salem, North Carolina until I was five. My father was a salesman at an awning company and my mother a receptionist for Sealtest. They'd gotten married when she was 16 and he 21. They were still young when my brother was born, and they named him Joe, after my father. Four years later they named me after the president who had just taken office again.

The summer I was five was when things started to split and sever. When I started to learn that boyhood wasn't just something you got because you had a house and a dog and a family. You had to earn it, or deserve it. You had to fight to hang on to it.

My mother taught me about my father's sins the way some mothers teach their kids the alphabet. *This is what he does, what he doesn't do, what he accuses me of* – all the time, as if she had no one else to tell it to. As if I understood what she was talking about. As if I didn't just stubbornly, stupidly, love him anyway, squirming in my chair, trying not to listen.

When they fight it makes a tension in the air so thick I imagine I can touch it. I want to slam my fist right through it and stop the shouting, bring them back. But I can't. All I can do is hang onto my mother's leg, crying, as she slams the door and locks him out. And then it's his fist that comes bursting through, his hairy knuckles shattering the window and unlocking the door so he can come storming in, demanding the entry that belongs to him. My mother is shouting and Sparky is barking and I'm crouched in the corner, all the fear in the room swirling together like a tornado so I can't tell whose is whose. They scream at each other and I wish I knew what makes them so unhappy. Why the life they have isn't enough, why this boy, this family, why nothing is working.

And when they're hugging suddenly, making up, I don't know what's real. I don't understand what made them stop any better than I know what made them start. So what should I believe in – their bodies pressed together, or the locked door dividing them and the glass he needed to break to get back in?

I'm still sobbing, so hard I can't catch my breath, and when my father picks me up and says *don't be scared* I want to become part of him, blend right in to his solid body. I want to bury my face in his chest and pretend this never happened. That it isn't already making holes in all of us. That even what is banished can be saved.

They packed us up and moved the family to Florida, trying, I guess, to save us. For two years I walked to school along the swamp, rode my *varoom* bike that sounded like a motorcycle, worked hard at just being a boy and not looking too closely at the people around me. But meanwhile my father was gambling his money away at the dog races, writing bad checks, chasing women, and when the accusations piled up as high as the empty beer cans and it didn't seem to make any difference, my mother took my brother and me and returned to North Carolina without him.

It took her another year to leave for real. I was seven when we left Florida, and when my father came back up to Winston-Salem to work for my uncle a year later, I got hopeful. Never mind that they were still fighting, never mind that he wasn't making his support payments or that my uncle and grandmother kept reminding my mother about his faults. They reminded her so much that she finally had him thrown in jail for not making the payments.

I'm going to see my father. That's what I'm thinking as I ride to the jail, in the back seat behind my mother and grandmother. Mom has a couple of beers in her. All I have in me is my hunger, my wishing, and it doesn't protect me the way the beer protects her. The two of them are telling each other what's wrong with my father, why he's been so bad to us. Someone should start listing my mother's sins because she's sure got some, but I keep quiet. I've got to concentrate on hoping for my father, concentrate the way you hold onto a can of Coke in the car, keeping it steady so it won't spill over and disappear.

When we get there they won't let me in. I have to wait in the car with my grandmother. I'm too full of sweaty tears and disappointment to let her comfort me. We wait and wait, my legs sticking to the seat of the car, and I try to picture what it's like in the jail. When I ask my grandmother, her answer makes me think of a kennel. I know how dogs look when they're locked in those cages and I wonder if that expression is on my father's face now.

Finally here comes my mother, striding over to us with her fury shimmering all around her. She yanks open the door of the car and even before she's inside she's telling my grandmother about it. *I let him have it!* she says, and she's not just angry but proud of herself. *I told him our marriage was a sham, I told him he never loved me —*

She finally doesn't need him, but she waited until he was locked up in a cage to tell him. When she says *I threw my ring at him!* I see that flinging in my mind, and I see that once you throw a wedding ring through the bars of a jail cell there's no getting it back.

Thrown, flung, gone. His face must be sad like a dog's, but maybe they're right, maybe he deserves to be in there. There is no side I can take without losing something. I start crying again, trying to make my mother notice me. Here I am in the back seat, and that's my father you're talking about.

"Your father won't be bothering us anymore," she says, and the pride in her voice has nothing to do with me. And so the secret forms inside me, molded solid by the heat and the tears and the realization that no one here knows my side: *I want him want him anyway doesn't matter what you say.* And from now on, whenever my mother tries to touch me, this hard defiant secret is what she feels.

Eventually I learned my mother's trick and learned it good. How to put a thick filter of beer and rage between myself and my own disappointment. But it was hard work, always having to smother the longing. I used to wonder if my brother had to work at it too, or if he just figured out way before I did that it was no use. When I think of Joe I think of him gone — always escaping the crossfire in a way I couldn't manage to. Where was he the day of the locked door and the broken window? Why wasn't he in the car with us on the way to the jail? He always seemed to figure he had better things to do than chase after my father or listen to my mother. He saved himself, but there must have been room for only one kid in that lifeboat, because when he escaped, he never took me with him.

"Where's my goddamn son?" my mother demanded when she called Joe's friends looking for him. Like he had no right to be anywhere else. I wanted to ask her in just that righteous tone, "Where's my goddamn father?" But I knew what she'd say. Not here, not here. And that was old news. I was 11 and it was three years since that visit to the jail, three years since we'd seen or heard from him. Joe was busy with school and sports and his friends whose houses he could disappear into until my mother went calling for him. But I was still hanging around dreaming of escape or rescue. Playing pirates in the woods by myself, running back and forth to act out both the good guys and the bad guys and see if I could finally figure out who was who.

Heading out through the tobacco fields to the woods, I hoped I'd find an animal's trail. I remembered what my Boy Scout manual taught me and I looked for broken twigs, prints in the mud. Signs of who had been here, clues to what had happened. Tracking what had gone on between my parents was nowhere near that easy. She saw one set of clues, he saw another, and I didn't know which ones to follow. When he sent for me the summer I was 11, invited me to come visit him in the junkyard in Florida where he was working, my mother figured I might as well go follow his trail for a while so I would finally understand that he was no good. When I got there, he spent the summer trying to talk me into his version of the story.

His version was that he had loved my mother, that she was the one who kicked him out. All the wrongs were hers. I should know he loved her, me, all of us, he shouldn't have to prove it.

I wanted proof anyway. After years of not seeing him, years of trying to remember that he loved me, I was ready for something I didn't have to work so hard to imagine. A father who was right there before my eyes. So I took it, a summer in his bare little room, sleeping on greasy sheets on the top bunk of his bed, ignoring the water bugs, slipping outside to play in the swamp with the alligator in it or climb on the stacks of cars. My version was that I was having a great time. The fact is I would have taken him any way he wanted me to, if I could just finally be his son.

"Why didn't Joe come?" he asked me one day.

"Why, would you rather have him than me?" I was fishing, waiting for him to say he loved me best.

"No, no, I was just wondering," he said, looking off into the distance, and I could see he was like me. Always wondering about the thing that didn't happen, the one who didn't want him. I didn't tell him Joe didn't come because he knew better. Because he had a life that was bigger than sitting around waiting for Dad to call. I wanted to think I was right, not stupid, I was getting something Joe was missing out on.

Like the *Playboy*s Dad had lying around. He didn't hide them any more than he hid the beer in the refrigerator. This was his life and welcome to it. If Joe wanted to see magazines up in Winston-Salem he would have to hide them from Mom, but here in Dad's junkyard room we were men together. He left the magazines out and he knew I liked them. "Hey, that was a long shower you took," he teased me every time, and it was the closest he ever came to saying *I know what it's like, I know how you feel.* It was the one time he ever got me absolutely right. This furious sweet pleasure I was discovering in my father's filthy shower was something we both understood.

I wondered if women understood it. If the beautiful girl across the road knew how I thought about her. If my aunt who yanked me away from my cousin when she found us under the steps years ago had ever been that curious herself.

At least my father got it. But it took him away from me, too. Wednesday nights he had a woman to go see, and he'd leave me with the beer as a babysitter. I watched him take a shower, shave his hairy face smooth, put on a clean shirt, slap on the cologne. After he left, the smell of his getting ready was still in the air, making everything seem possible. I took a beer from the refrigerator, felt the cold bottle in my hand. By the time I went outside into the heavy Florida air it was working in me, making me feel what he felt. I climbed on top of the cars and told myself this was the best game I could play. At the top of that mountain, looking out over the junkyard and the swamp, feeling the beer loosen my muscles, I could say I was having a wonderful time.

And so they passed, a whole summer of Wednesdays, him disappearing for his dates with a waitress and me waiting at home with what he'd left me.

"When are you gonna get a bigger place so I can come live with you?"

"When I win the Trifecta."

Never, in other words. Because the way his luck was going, I couldn't see it happening. Maybe it bothered him that I didn't say it's OK Dad, this junkyard shack is good enough for me. But I didn't need a mansion. I just wanted him to have a life I didn't have to squeeze my way into. To live somewhere that looked like it was meant to have a boy in it. I wanted him to say I'll make it happen, son, I'll do anything, I'll find a way to have you with me.

He didn't say that. But when he drove me back to Winston-Salem at the end of the summer, he told me he'd see me again. That fall he called me more than he ever had. Each time I took the phone from my mother I felt the little triumph: see, he *is* calling. See, I was right to go down there, right to keep hoping for him.

After a few months the calls started to taper off. I'd come home and ask my mother, and she'd tell me no, he hadn't called, and I'd turn away, feeling the flat metallic taste of disappointment in my mouth. And embarrassment, too, because she'd caught me wanting him.

I'd gone to spend a summer with him and I'd come back to my mother's, and now whose kid was I going to be? I could believe what she said or what he said. I could blame the beer in her hand or the one in his, could feel jealous of the sailor I caught her kissing or the waitress he left me for those Wednesdays. But it was impossible to know which story was right. Did he want to leave, did she push him away, did *I* push him away?

Things happen. People explain them the way they want to, or don't explain at all. They give you pieces and leave you to figure it out, and so the story that sticks is the story you make, the story you tell yourself, but you're no more aware of it than you're aware of making your own bones. They just grow, layer after layer, the interpretations and conclusions getting bred right in.

This is what a child is made of: the things he believes are true. It doesn't matter what other people think they're doing, what reasons they have, whether they mean to be bad or good. To understand, you have to go back to that boy and the way that *he* tried to make sense of it all, the explanations *he* manufactured, because those are what stay with him long after the other people are gone.

Spring in North Carolina: the weeds high, maple leaves blazing green and spilling out from the woods onto the roads, vines crawling over the cars left out in the fields. It's a landscape of abundance and abandon, excess and neglect. I'm on my own in it, 12 years old, my bicycle carrying me from school to Pee Wee football practice and from there to my job at the gas station where I earn 95 cents an hour and a weekly box of bubble gum. The money makes me feel grown up, and changing tires and washing cars makes me strong. I've almost stopped expecting my father to call.

"Keep the change," the man says, with a diffidence I don't yet recognize as calculation. I've seen him before, leaning against his car and watching my football games, but I haven't given more thought to him than I'd give to any fortyish working stiff with a potbelly and cigarettes rolled into his shirtsleeve. He looks as ordinary as someone's father. And he knows that's exactly the ordinariness I want.

That night at the gas station, he offers to give me a ride to my uncle's beer joint. He knows that's where I go when I leave. He's come by often enough to learn these facts of my life, and when he says, "I'm going that way anyway," I believe him. I put my bike in the trunk of his car and climb in the front seat next to him. Nothing makes me suspicious until I realize he's not heading in the right direction. I ask where he's going, but the fear isn't sharp yet; it's only a dim shape hovering in the distance. I barely know enough to recognize it – nobody warned me about this kind of danger. "Oh, I'm just going this way," he reassures me. "Don't worry, I'll come around the back." I sit in limbo, not sure what to believe.

He stops the car on a quiet road. There's nothing around us except the shadows that the moonlight makes of the trees. "Check the trunk," he suggests. "I think it's open on your bike." I get out, glad of the warning, and he follows. Before I have time to realize that the trunk isn't open, I'm slammed against it and he's ripping my pants down.

My mind is not big enough for what he is doing to me. It is not something I ever imagined one man could do to another. Does he see something in me that lets him know I deserve this? Or did he decide to take me and make me into what he is? My hands are flat against the hood of the trunk, my bike is inside but unreachable. It was my bike that got me out of the car, got me to do what he asked.

And then, as suddenly as he finishes, his hands are on my throat, his voice distant through my fear but filling me up, obliterating everything else I've known: "Better not tell, or I'll break your neck like a chicken." And filling my mind, now, the memory of the chickens on my grandfather's farm, slaughtered in one easy motion, helpless in the hands of the greedy. Their necks snapped as they surrendered whatever power they had. They yielded to a world that had no mercy.

I grab my bike and ride away, the gravel crunching under my wheels, dust flying as I pedal harder. My heart is pounding along with the crickets who mock me as I go by. My legs still carry me; my body still gets me there. But the tears fall against my will. As I get close to my uncle's, I rub my arm across my eyes, removing the evidence.

In the bar, everything is the same as always. My eyes adjust to the red light, my ears to the chatter of the people at the tables. Somewhere among them is my mother, bending down to serve them, laughing along. My uncle leans over the bar, his huge belly resting on it. No one notices that I'm late or even that I've arrived at all. I won't look to them for answers. There is something new in me now, something that no one sees. I'm standing among these people but I don't live here anymore. I have gone to an unimaginable place.

Soon my uncle looks up and calls me over. He says something that I don't hear, but I know the mocking tone. His hand comes up to smack me, and I duck but don't escape the sting. I want to say, "Don't you realize what just happened to me?" I look at his huge moon face and realize there is no one to tell, anyway, even if I dared to risk that broken chicken neck. For a minute I think about my grandmother at home, but I know I can't ask her to hear this – it's too big, too bad, it's too much to ask. Look around: there is no one. My uncle is out of the question. My mother, coming through the crowd now on her high heels, can't even stop her own brother from hurting me, so how can she protect me from anyone else? How can I ask her to make me feel safe?

And I know now that my father will never call.

Spring turns to summer and then to fall. In this unimaginable place where I now live, I drink, I try every drug offered to me, I steal my mother's car and get arrested for speeding. "Why did you do it?" my mother asks after she picks me up from the jail. "I wanted to go to the beach," I tell her, as though that is any kind of answer. I can't say: I'm trying to signal you from exile. I have no idea how to get back.

Years later, when I'm robbing someone and using a knife, I'm still doing it from exile, still trying to signal in this choking, garbled way. I understand terror, but I don't let anyone know I understand it. I just use it. I show people their own blood, their own fear, their own weakness. What fools they are to think they have any control over what happens to them. They can only yield, over and over again, to hands that have no mercy.

This is the story I keep telling, in such crude and impossible language, to an audience that is either too terrified or too preoccupied to hear.

It would have been easier if he had dragged me into the car, held a gun to my head, left me nothing about myself I could blame. But I'd climbed in willingly. I was glad not to have to bike home, and flattered that this man was taking a little extra trouble over me.

Yeah, I wanted someone to take the trouble. That's what got me climbing into the car: my hunger. An emptiness he must have been able to *see,* because he knew there'd be room for him there. And that was as shameful as what he'd done to me. From now on, I would keep both secrets. I wouldn't tell what happened that night, and I wouldn't tell how much I wanted people, either.

That's the mistake, see – letting it show. Better to put an angry expression on your face than to let your mother see how much you want her to wrap you in her arms and promise that everything will be all right. What good's a hug you have to beg for, anyway? Stay still and tight and wait to see if she ever reaches for you herself. See if paying attention is ever her own idea.

That spring that I was 12, she was going out with a guy named Grady. She met him at the beer joint when he came in to play cards. He was a gambler like my father, but the difference was he kept winning. He was tall, quiet, a little mysterious. He'd done time for bootlegging, way back before we knew him. He seemed ready to do a lot to win my mother over, maybe even to win me over too. If she stayed with him, he might end up taking me places and coming to my football games.

Did I want that? Or did I want him to go away so I could have my mother all to myself? I was too tangled up to know. And then it all happened fast. They disappeared one weekend and came back married. "Come in and say hello to your new stepfather," she announced. Her happiness filled up the whole house, filled it the way her anger always did. I kicked the door, helpless and outraged. I wasn't ready. I hadn't even figured out what I was hoping for.

"He'll get used to it," my mother was saying to Grady, nodding to him over my head. She was reassuring him, but I knew I was supposed to get the message too. In the end it doesn't much matter what you've figured out, or what you wish for. In the end there wasn't much more room for me in their house than there had been at my father's. Nights when they sat at the kitchen table after work, they drew a curtain of alcohol around themselves and stayed inside it. It kept me out even when I was right there in the room with them. I sat watching them, nursing the longing I would never let them see.

Grady had been around a while when I got picked up for stealing my mother's car the first time. They came to the station to get me and Grady looked at me and shook his head. "I don't know what the hell's wrong with you, boy," was all he said.

What was wrong would have taken a long time to explain, longer than they ever seemed to have. Can you get to the bottom of a kid's troubles in less than the time it takes to drink a six-pack? Less than the time it takes to yell at him? Less than the time it took to get into those troubles in the first place?

I will say this for Grady: he did try. Tried to get my mother to lay off me, anyway. "All right, you made your point," he'd tell her. "Now leave the kid alone." He knew how she had to grind a point into the dirt before she'd let up. He could try to get her to go easier on me, be lighter with the rules or the criticizing. But he couldn't make her want to touch me, couldn't force her to look at me and like what she saw. There are limits even to what a decent man can do when he steps into the story of someone else's life.

I have to show them. They leave their doors unlocked and I have to show them how stupid that is. Or they put their trust in fancy security systems and I have to show that even that doesn't work. I can get in anyway.

You break into a house and enter it. You break their trust and enter their private lives, you break the rules and enter into new ones that only make sense years later, when you come to understand that you were broken, you were entered and invaded, the thieving had already begun.

People think they know how to hide things, but I can sit in the middle of a room and figure out the place they'd choose, and most of the time I'm right. I can find it: the money, the jewelry, the naked pictures they took of each other. The other guys are racing through the house, trying to get something good and get out fast, but I'm taking my time, lying on the bed, making a sandwich, trying to feel how it would be to live these lives. I search for things I'm not going to take, just for the feeling of going through the drawers and tossing things around the room. I picture the people coming home and seeing everything changed. They'll understand that their perfect world isn't so perfect after all.

The first time someone comes home and finds me in the house, I'm by myself, standing in the bedroom, and I hear a woman's voice call "Robert, come in here!" She's halfway to me already – I never even heard the front door open. I bolt for the door and as I pass her my arm smacks her throat, throwing her against the wall. I hear her husband asking, "Honey, what happened?" just before I clear the front door, running.

What will she tell him? How will she describe the stranger she saw, the feeling of coming home and finding him there, the spill of her belongings on the floor, the way the kid's arm felt as it knocked against her throat? Will she be able to tell her husband all about it, will she cry in his arms, or will the words have been choked out of her too? Will she picture that kid at night as she's falling asleep? Will she ever be able to forget him?

This boy goes places he isn't supposed to go. He goes in and takes what doesn't belong to him. Is he just bad? Does he not know right from wrong? Is it a sure thing that this boy breaking into houses at 12 and 13 and 14 is going to end up in prison at 21?

Maybe prison will teach him a lesson. Trouble is, he's learned a whole lot of lessons already. There are things he knows, and those things are driving him now. Driving the thieving the way they will later drive the violence, in ways it's going to take him years to understand.

Racing away from the house, clutching whatever it was in my hand, I could feel the thrill: hey, this is *mine!* I took it! How amazing that you can just take something and suddenly it doesn't belong to the owner anymore.

Most things we took, we sold as soon as we could. Or we just got rid of them, like the guns we stole and then buried in the woods. But sometimes I held onto something small, like a coin from someone's collection, and in my fist or my pocket it gave off power for a while, burning with the memory of where I'd been. It was proof of what I could do, could take, could have. And then one day I'd look down and there wasn't any kind of magic in it anymore. It wore off, just like the magic of drugs always did, just like any of the fraudulent promises of relief or power.

The arithmetic of stealing seems simple: subtract from one person and add to another. But the internal equations are much more complex than that. It's all about settling a score. Something's been taken from me and that gives me the right to take from these people who obviously have way too much, because *everyone* else has way too much. I'm the one with the missing place, the emptiness, and what I grab from this house isn't mine but maybe it should be. Or maybe everything I want is by definition too much, because I don't really deserve anything, so I've got to get what I can in secret, on the sly.

"Jesus Christ, you want *another?*" my uncle exclaimed every time I squirted Coke into a glass from his fountain or got my mother to ask him for a bowl of his spaghetti sauce. I liked it enough to want it even though it was his. But he never offered first, and when he handed me the bowl it was with a resentment so thick I'm surprised I could taste the sauce through it.

He got me a dog one time and the happiness flared up inside me in that dumb perpetual way that a kid's happiness does even when he ought to know better. Red, my Irish Setter, waiting for me under my grandmother's willow every day when I came home from school. Just when I got so I counted on the sight of him there, he was gone. My uncle sold him to a guy he knew. Just went ahead and sold a kid's dog without apology. Nothing I have, nothing I care for, is really mine to keep. He could take my dog, he could complain about every penny I cost him, and he could smack me on the back of the head and call me *punk* and it didn't matter if people were watching or if I told him to stop.

Later, I found out how to make people stop. I found out what works. It was after my grandmother's death, after I had left home to live with Tom the drug dealer. We were going to find someone who owed money to Tom, and I can still hear the contempt in the man's voice when I demanded the money.

"You ain't nothin' but a punk kid."

"Keep talking," I say, "and this punk kid will shoot you in the head."

"Don't pull that gun out," Tom tells me, but I'm pulling it out already, and in the same moment the guy is saying "He's got a gun?"

"You're fucking right," I answer. I'm handling this and I know what I'm doing. Tom is standing there surprised and the guy is trying to look scornful but he's scared now. He hands over the money.

He handed it over because that's what guns do. They turn a punk kid into someone whose orders get followed. He called me a punk kid and my uncle's fat moon face rose in front of my eyes and I could hear his voice saying *hey punk* and I could feel his hand smacking against my head and I wanted some way to tell the world not to call me that anymore. Afterwards, Tom asked me if I would really have shot the guy and I said yes. "I'm not letting him take anything from you," I told him, and the fury came from way before I'd ever met Tom.

Anger is partly about weariness. It's about saying you've had enough and you're going to put a stop to this any way you can. All those times you couldn't do anything didn't do anything just let it happen. So much gets taken and then there comes a time when you say *no more,* even though what really matters is gone and the guns and knives don't bring it back.

"I can get beer," I say to them. My offering, my ticket, my way in.

"How can a little kid like you get beer?"

Well, I wasn't so little. At 12 I was the youngest at any party but I had my uncle's beer, cases of it. All the days I helped him unload it, all the thanks I never got, all the smacking and insults and grudgingly given food. It was easy to wait for the moment his head was turned, throw a case out the door, and hide it behind a tree until Kenny came by to pick it up.

Kenny was Cherokee and I thought he was the coolest guy around. He walked barefoot, even in winter, and he flicked his long hair back as he talked. His eagle profile stared out at the world, taking it all in, and I imagined he felt himself as apart and alone as I did. He was four years older than me and I was just glad he let me hang out with him.

"My brother's coming back from Vietnam," Kenny announced one day. This brother of his, Lane, was the first guy I really noticed who'd been in Vietnam, but if Lane had brought back any battle scars, we couldn't see them. All he admitted to bringing back were canisters of heroin and mescaline. Kenny told me about it soon after Lane came home and asked if I wanted to do some.

How did the stakes go up so fast? I'd never even smoked grass and here we were talking about becoming junkies. But with Kenny, my credo had to be *never flinch*. I had to go along with anything, and I did. I agreed to try the heroin.

He was a magician, doing some kind of mysterious fussing with the needle and talking to me all the while. "You want to do this, right?" As if he was giving me a chance to reconsider instead of digging me in deeper. *Never flinch*. To keep him, to prove myself, to *reassure* myself, I would do whatever it took.

All I felt that first time was sick, puking sick, and I didn't see what was so great about it. But the second time I started to get the idea. Lane thought it was hilarious to watch a 12-year-old get whacked. He burst out laughing when I sat there saying, "Wow!" like a caricature of a kid on drugs, or when I asked him if we could do it again, eager as a puppy.

Sometimes I'd come home and look at my straight brother, with his good grades and praise from the teachers and his ability to get out without taking this path – I'd look at him and think *you have no idea*. But he didn't care that he left me behind. It was clearly every man for himself, and I'd get out in my own way.

If you step onto that dark path, is there any way to come back? Was I a junkie because I'd agreed to try Kenny's magic? Was I homosexual because of what a man had done with me? Was I evil because of all the things I let happen?

Do we change ourselves or do the things that happen to us change us?

By the time I was 13 or 14, the drugs and the parties were routine. My mother stopped working at my uncle's, so I hardly ever went over there and I couldn't get beer that way anymore. I was still working at the gas station, but that didn't bring in anywhere near the money we needed. I learned how to steal from people's empty houses, and then I learned that Kenny and Lane knew another way to get money.

Sex is always some kind of mystery. By now I knew well enough how a body could want another. But the things some people would do for desire! I wondered sometimes, was everyone a pervert under the surface? Robbing those nice houses, I'd find vibrators and naked pictures hiding in the drawers, not so far from the Bible, and I'd think about how there was so much people never talked about or explained. Explain to me why everyone turns out to have a secret. Explain to me how Kenny and Lane could do what they did to get money for beer, and do it so casually I almost didn't catch on.

They said we could go rob the gays who hung around by the bus station. They made it sound easy, but I wasn't in any hurry to find out if they were right. Robbing an empty house was one thing; going right up to someone and robbing him in person seemed another game entirely. They said *we'll take care of it,* and I sat waiting in the car. But as I watched them go and return, things didn't add up. How could they be coming back in the same car they got into? How could they be calling out good-byes to a man they'd robbed? How could they return next week to the same guy when even I knew to stay clear of anyone I'd robbed?

"So what?" they said when I confronted them. "Yeah, they ask to suck your dick too – what about it?"

They acted like it had nothing to do with them. So you had to sit in a guy's car and let him put his mouth on you? And worry that you might like it, or worry that if you *didn't* like it, he wouldn't pay you? I couldn't see it, couldn't imagine voluntarily getting into one of those cars. But one day on the way over, Lane said, "It's your turn, you do it this time."

"Fuck that," I tried, but it was too late to start flinching now.

"You'll let *us* do it," Kenny said. "You'll drink the beer but you won't contribute. That's not fair."

The message was clear: I had to pull my own weight. Lane explained what to do. We got to the bus station and a car cruised past Lane, looked at us, blinked its lights, and Lane blinked back, returning the signal.

Even in the car with the guy, I kept trying to put it off. *In a minute, in a minute*, I said until finally I held my breath and jumped off the twisted diving board and let him do what he wanted. In a way I was glad I hated it. I could reassure myself this didn't turn me on, I wasn't gay, the man at the gas station hadn't changed me.

Of course, he had. Changed me. The next few times we went back to the bus station I brought a screwdriver with me. If any of them got rough with me I was going to have protection this time. It didn't really matter that they didn't, that I never needed to use the weapon. I'd learned by now how men thought about boys, how they wanted them for their own sick reasons, or didn't want them and left them behind. I'd seen that whether they paid money or threatened to break your neck or stopped calling because they had other things to do, whatever they did would always be, thoroughly, for themselves.

Why does summer promise so much and deliver so little? The sun bakes the mud in our fields to a deep, glowing red; my grandmother's willow bends low enough to scrape the earth. Nights when the guys come to get me, we ride around drinking cheap wine and the smell of other people's barbecues trails us, coating the air. August is heavy and full but it seems I always come up short.

If the beer bottles sit out on the table long enough, they start to sweat, and if my mother sits drinking them long enough, she'll show me who she really is. "I think I'll have a cool one," she says when she comes home. Yeah, Mom, it's hot out, go ahead. Just don't think you're fooling anyone. Soon enough she says, "I think I'll have another." And another and another, and I'm just watching, waiting for the monster to come out. I wish I could be one of those kids who can count on things finishing exactly the way they start out. But my mother starts out a woman who comes home from work and just happens to want a cool drink, and she ends up glassy-eyed, facing me with a look I can't believe anyone's supposed to call *mother*.

"You know what?" she says, and I brace myself. "You look just like your father."

My father, the guy I haven't seen in four years. There's no way I can untangle the mixture of terror and pride and longing and spite that rises up in me when she says this. I just take it all and pack it hard, into something I can throw right back.

"I am." I turn my face to her so she can see. "Just fucking like him. That's why you hate me so much."

And she doesn't contradict me.

Grady sometimes tries to undo the damage. "Don't listen to that, son," he says in the quiet after the storm. "What she's saying isn't true." He'll stick up for me only when it's safe; he doesn't want her to turn on him either. He's saying this stuff *now*, but I think of him sitting mute at the table while she lashed out at me. What I want to know is, why doesn't anyone, just anyone, do the right thing at the right time?

Boone's Farm Apple Wine is the cheapest and most disgusting stuff they've got. You can slap down a dollar and get a bottle, if you feel like paying, but the bottles are kept close to the door and they're easy to steal.

"Why did I drink that?" you laugh as you try to spit out the aftertaste. But soon enough you're asking, "Where's that other bottle?" He hands it to you and you drink it down. It softens the edges, like the moon on those nights when it blurs right into the sky. For a little while, there's not so much difference between you and the rest of the world.

She drank beer; I drank wine. We weren't the same: I hated beer. I wasn't the miserable fuck she was. Is the difference clear?

Nights when I'm not too wasted myself, I come home and then turn right around to go out looking for her. There aren't too many places she can be. They all smell of stale smoke and beer that will never wash out of the carpet.

I find her in one of them, alone because she and Grady have had a fight. I tell her it's time to come home.

"I'm not going," she says with that belligerence drunks always think sounds like strength.

"Come on," I urge her, and she finally does. On the way she yells at me, or she tells me she loves me. It comes to the same thing these days. Even the good things that happen are just too late, long past due. I'm 15, she's 35, and it may be too late for me to believe her.

Sometimes she has to come find me. I never call her unless I have to, unless a cop makes me or calls her himself. These days I get picked up for little things: driving underage, taking her car, stealing asthma pills and passing them off as speed. People buy them but I finally get caught selling in a diner in Virginia. They have nothing to hold me on, though, once they realize the pills really are Primatene, just like I told them. So they let me go, but I have to call my mother to come get me.

Some kids are scared when they get in trouble and know their mother's going to find out. The clearest thing I feel as I wait for her is spite. *Now you're going to find out*, I think to myself. *You'll find out how it feels to have your life disrupted. You'll have some trouble you won't be able to hush up.*

When I said it then, it came out mean. Years later, when I think about that phrase *now you're going to find out*, it can sound like a twisted kind of hope.

She picks me up and she's furious — at the embarrassment, at the trouble I put *her* to, at my friends whose fault this obviously is.

"It's those damn kids you hang around with."

It's always the damn kids. Not me, not her, not this life we don't know how to live. She doesn't look at anything straight on. And so I keep disappearing, taking off without telling her where, not coming home for days.

"I'm sick of it," she says when I finally do come home. "You're never here, you never call."

"If you didn't make me feel so fucking miserable –" I pronounce each word carefully, like it's a lesson she's been told a hundred times and never learned. "I wouldn't have to leave."

She shakes her head. "Maybe your uncle was right. I should have sent you away."

"Maybe he was. Maybe you should have."

There's nothing she can say about me that I don't already know.

My grandmother hated that I disappeared, too. When she asked why, I told her I just wanted to get away. I had more gentleness for her than I had for my mother, because somehow I knew she was trying. She didn't say anything after that, and in her silence was the recognition that things weren't always so great for me at home. But I'd look at her and even as I willed her to understand more, I'd know how impossible that was. How do you tell the grandmother who once held you close at night that you can't stay because you've got drugs to do, girls to screw, that you've got a knife and know how to use it? I was way too old for that kind of closeness anyway. I'd need more than the feel of her flannel nightgown to make me safe.

It's late afternoon at the end of the summer, and I pass my grandmother as she's working in her garden.

"Why don't you come and see me more often?" She leans against the hoe, looking at me.

Why? Because the distance would be too far to travel. Because it's too hard to bear how she sees me but only halfway, how she wants something from me I can't give: reassurance that I'm all right. It's not enough anymore, to sit in her living room listening to the rain on the tin roof of the porch.

I make an excuse and head out for another night with the guys in the neighborhood, passing bottles in the parking lot by the bowling alley, riding home and stopping to puke by the side of the road. Falling into bed, not going out to look for Mom this time even though she isn't home.

Morning comes but I don't see it. It's noon before I'm awake, and it's late afternoon before I realize we haven't heard from Grandma all day. I look out the window of the trailer and see her car there, the house dark.

The door is locked when I get there, and a hint of worry flickers up my spine. She's always got the door open to let the air in. There's no answer when I knock, so I crawl through the window, run to her room. There she is on the bed, lying with her arms outstretched, eyes wide and unblinking. Such a strange position, and her body is so cold under my hands.

My mother comes running in. She must have been right behind me.

"Grandma's not waking up," I say, the way a child would say it.

Mom's already crying. She stares at her mother's body for a moment, then turns to me wildly and speaks the words I'll never forget.

"Well, you won't have your grandmother to run to anymore."

Is this what grief is, this ice that rips people even farther apart? When the will is read, most of her personal possessions are left to me. I win: she loved me best. But it's such a bitter victory, sawdust in my mouth. Even the realization that my grandmother never gave up on me comes too late for me to let it make the difference. What I'm left with in the raw and barren days after her death isn't her faith in me, but my mother's response, quick and brutal, telling me that even the meager haven my grandmother's house had offered me was more than I deserved. I look around at the people who are left and realize there's nothing here for me. It's time to quit. My mother regrets not sending me away? I'll do it for her. I've practically done it already.

How do you reach a kid in trouble? So many years after that summer, I stand facing a kid I work with. He yells "Get the fuck away from me!" and I know he really means *come closer*. I know it because when I look at him I see the wild terror, the furious desire to escape his own skin, and it's as familiar as my own. I know how much he wants someone to see him, reach him, save him, and how much he hates that wanting because all it ever comes to is more disappointment. Some days it seems he *is* that disappointment, and more than anything he wants to shuck it off, pretend he doesn't want what he can't have. He yells because today is one of those days he can't bear it. Now that I'm the man standing with him, I try to show him how to bear it. I try to hold on even when he wants to shake me off too.

Now, with years of thinking about this and having other people help me think about it, I can turn my mother's anger around in my mind and see that from another angle it looks like despair. She saw me slip away like she'd seen my father slip away and she didn't know what to do about it. When she called Joe and said, "Your brother's left, I don't know what's wrong with him," she wanted sympathy but maybe she also wanted help. Grady tried to soften my mother's sharp tongue, and my grandmother tried to get me to come visit her. In a way, these ineffectual tries are what snag my memory the most. They just didn't add up to enough. Not for me, not then. They felt like too little too late, or they felt slippery, not solid – either inconsistent or outright fake. The words "I love you" spoken through a haze of beer slid right through me without sticking. What was real? How did I know the kindness wouldn't turn out to be a set-up? I could never relax into it; I had to brace myself for what always came next.

And maybe their efforts weren't enough because none of them knew how much trouble I really was in – inside myself and out. Maybe I just needed them to try harder because I was already that far away.

It's tempting to say *well, you needed too much*. But who's to say what's too much for anyone? Was it too much to ask that my mother realize I might miss my father? That she tell me she love me without having to get drunk first? That we grieve together for my grandmother? That she might have looked at me the night I came home three years before, and realize something had happened to mark me forever?

You see how easy it is to hate wanting. The list could be enormous, all the things wanted and not gotten, some not even imagined. If it really was all right to want so much, then you have to face the disappointment, in all its monstrous gaping horror. You have to learn to grieve for it, just like you have to learn to grieve for the dead instead of turning every loss into rage.

A kid in trouble is always daring other people to reject him, because he's so sure that's what's going to happen anyway. But a kid in trouble is also always daring other people to accept him: to see through his cover, understand him the way an adult is supposed to understand a child. Somehow he can't just say it outright. Something chokes the words, so he says it every other way he can and waits for them to figure it out. And when they don't, he assumes it's because they aren't trying. Or because he's not worth the effort.

As my grandmother's willow scattered leaves everywhere, summer gave way to an impossible fall. I didn't leave right away. Even though I knew better, for a little while after the funeral I tried to be a regular boy: eating oatmeal cookies, watching TV, listening when my mother told me not to go out at night. I thought maybe this was what my grandmother wanted and maybe I could pull it off. But nothing changed: not the nightly beer, not the accusations, not the chill look in my mother's eyes. Nothing protected us from the disappointment we felt when we faced each other. In the cramped hallway of the trailer, we stood so close I could see the pores of her face, and I reached out and grabbed the finger she was pointing at me. Grabbed it and held it and felt my anger close in around it.

One day that fall I'm sitting on my bed cleaning my gun. Mom and Grady don't know I keep knives, but this gun's no secret, it's just a country kid's gun like everyone has around here, for shooting squirrels and rabbits. I'm cleaning it, trying not to hear them fighting on the other side of the wall. But the trying takes so much energy. To block them out I have to block myself out too. I feel dizzy, like there's nothing to hold me down.

Suddenly she's right outside my door.

"I hate your fucking guts!" she yells. To Grady? To me? I can't tell but it doesn't even matter. It's just the same hatred, ricocheting off the walls, and I'm so tired of it. I start loading the gun and I'm not thinking anything, just feeling how tired I am and how much I don't want to be this boy in this house with this life.

"I'm sick of you," I say, and she hears my voice and turns around. Yes, it's me, that invisible kid in the other room.

"I'm going to kill you." I've got the gun ready now.

She looks right at me and says, "Go ahead, shoot me."

Does she think I won't? Does she wish I would? My hands are gripping the gun but I couldn't say what's going to happen next. It feels like this is happening to someone else.

"Son," Grady says quietly, from the doorway. "You need to put that gun down. That won't solve anything."

"Yes, it will!" There's desperation underneath the anger. I don't want to hear what won't solve anything, I want to hear what *will*.

He doesn't argue. Neither of them says another word; they just stand frozen, and so do I. And then somehow the moment is gone, the adrenaline already leaking out of me. I lower the gun.

"You ain't fucking worth it," I say as I let the bullet shells fall to the floor.

I've never in my life felt so alone.

The aloneness. If you could look into that trailer and see the boy with the gun pointed at his mother, it would scare you, the way he looks as if he really will do it, the way the adults stand immobilized in the doorway, the way the echoes of every hateful word still linger in the air around them. You would see his cold fury: all the times she's looked at him like she wants to wipe him off the planet now reflected in his own pupils. But would you see the despair, filling his body so totally that he fears he'll float away?

I came that close to pulling the trigger, and even as the panic receded I knew I had crossed some kind of line. I told myself that next time I wouldn't be such a coward. Next time I had that much power, I wouldn't hesitate. I didn't ask myself why I was so sure there would be a next time, but of course there was. Not with my mother – I got out, got far enough away, that I never had to come that close again. But the feelings of that day were always with me. Life just kept being about exile. I kept learning how much farther I could go and how impossible it seemed to get back.

Now I wonder if grief might be a way back. Not the icy grief of that time, but a grief that actually thaws out the heart. I sit here as a grown man wishing I could go back to that day and find some other way out, or some other way to speak to her. Some way that would have actually set us on the road to repairing our broken love instead of severing me more fully from her and from myself. It's a wish I can't have. But slowly I discover that even the wishing restores something to me, something I hardly know if I can describe. It's the part of me that sees what brought those people to that moment. The part that can tell this story to someone else without either rage or apology, just with sadness for the boy, for the family, for everything they'd take back or do differently if they could.

We called him Uncle Tom, this middle-aged man who was nobody's uncle. He had a kid's eager face and a scientist's fascination with what happens when you mix two chemicals together. In his basement lab he created MDA, the drug everyone wanted, the drug that years later would be called Ecstasy. We called it the love drug, but it wasn't love that propelled me up to Tom's doorstep and it wasn't love that kept me there with him for almost a year.

A year, my God. A year of what? The memory shimmers and blurs and I realize nothing was what it seemed then. Tom's house was a way out of my own house but not the way I really needed. His MDA offered power and freedom and an end to the choking misery. Except that somehow, when the year was over, I was no better off. In fact, I was worse off, and so were a lot of other people.

MDA was like nothing I'd tried before, and I'd tried just about everything. The unbelievable explosive rush at the start, melting into a high that could last as long as twelve hours. It heightened everything so you could believe you were alive with sensation, even as it obliterated every other feeling you had. I wanted it, enough to ring this strange man's bell and risk the consequences.

"Are you Uncle Tom?" I asked when he opened the door.

"Depends on who's asking," he answered, taking a careful look at me.

Who *was* asking? What did he see in that kid standing there? In my worst moments now I imagine that he took one look and saw everything. That he knew exactly what was missing in me and figured out how he could pretend to supply it. But all I knew then was that he intrigued me: this guy in his forties running a huge drug operation by himself. How had he figured it out? How much experimenting down in that lab had it taken? I was curious about everything, and when he let me in and started answering my questions, I didn't want to leave. After a while he asked where I lived, who my family was, and I told him I didn't want to go home.

"You can't stay here," he warned me, sounding like any stern adult trying to ward off a kid's demands. When he ended up letting me stay, he let me think he was doing me the favor. Let me feel I was the one who owed him something.

Tom didn't take anything by force. There were no hands around my neck, no threats I could recognize. But he must have seen that he could use me for himself, and do it by a sleight of mind so smooth I'd think I'd done the deciding. What Tom wanted was young boys and the illusion that they wanted him too. And the illusion that we were all praying to the same deity: holy MDA, the drug that lay its silky net of absolution over everything, taking all the bad memories away and leaving a pure and seductive rapture in their place. Who wouldn't pray to a god like that?

Who wouldn't? I wonder now. There must have been kids in that town who didn't need oblivion coursing through their veins. There must have been kids still whole and unclaimed, kids who could go home again. He must have seen right away that I wasn't one of them.

He didn't take anything by force, but he took nonetheless. The first time, he had me lie on the bed with the fan blowing a cool breeze over my body. "Isn't the bed comfortable?" he asked softly as the drug began to take hold. "Doesn't the fan feel good?" Slow and sure, he took the experience and arranged it for me, calling my attention to every sensation until I lost track of whose idea each feeling had been. It was easy for him to move on to "How about if I do this?", laying his hands on my leg, my back, gradually touching everywhere, and didn't it all just seem part of the experience? Wasn't it easy to convince myself that MDA made any sensation an OK sensation to have?

Except I couldn't. Even MDA couldn't completely erase the crawling discomfort I felt at being touched by a man three times my age. I tried. I tried to like it or at least tolerate it, in case it was part of the deal, something I had to do to keep Tom happy. And maybe what he was doing was really OK after all, which would mean I wasn't as dirty as I had felt all this time. Maybe everything was fine, smooth and mellow and fine, and the gut-clenching anxiety I felt as his hands pierced the oblivion and made me feel 12 and helpless all over again, was only in my imagination ... no, not quite. I couldn't talk myself into it. I told Tom I couldn't and he didn't push me. For years I thought that made him different from the real abuser.

He didn't take anything by force. No, he just moved in on that empty place inside me and planted his own flag there, leaving me a little less *me* than I had before.

There's a place in people, the soft center of need or fear. You can see it in their eyes when you have something they want, or when they see you flick open a knife, or during sex when desire crashes over them and they let themselves go under. This place repelled me but it fascinated me too. Ever since the rapist found it in me and claimed it, I kept trying to find it in other people. And each time I did, I felt the thud of recognition: *there it is. That's the feeling*. It's not that I *liked* seeing it, exactly. But I was drawn to it again and again. I'd watch the surrender in someone else's eyes and stay smugly in control, as if none of it had anything to do with me. As if I could convince myself that we had divided things up: they took all the weakness and fear and left me with only strength and power.

It wasn't true, of course. But as an illusion, it was seductive as hell. It meant that when Tom asked me if I wanted to sell the drug for him, I jumped at the chance. Real power, for the first time! I would have what everyone wanted and they would have to come asking for it.

And they did. Guys I hadn't heard from in years called up. Beautiful girls wanted to be near me. If fifteen or twenty kids chipped in and got $600 together, that would buy them an ounce: eight or even twelve hours of blissful oblivion for all of them. Twenty kids each time who all wanted what I had, and the money added up. I became Tom's cash machine, doling out the money he asked for, buying myself whatever I wanted. I was right at the center. I didn't need anything.

Other kids came over to join the party. They came for the drug, and if Tom had other ideas, well, that wasn't exactly my problem. I was glad he was leaving me alone now, and who knows – maybe some of the guys who ended up in Tom's bed actually liked what happened there. Tom didn't have to spell it out for me. "Who's that?" he asked me when he saw someone he liked. "Why don't you invite him over?" And I would.

"See if Mike wants to come back," he'd say afterwards, and he didn't have to spell that out either. I'd run it past the guy, testing whether he was OK with what had happened or whether it bothered him enough that he wouldn't come back. The question was a lot more interesting to me than I let on. *Did* these guys mind? Were they ashamed? Was this a bad thing to do, or not? I would have been grateful for an answer. What was the right way to feel? Show me, interpret it for me, this experience that has no name, this memory I don't know how to carry. But the interpretation was always blurred; it was impossible to read because no one talked about it straight out. Some acted as though what happened with Tom didn't count any more than anything else that happened in that house. And a kid who didn't like it might stay away, but he never talked about it so I never got to hear him say *this feels wrong*.

That whole year, I didn't have to think about anything. I believed what I told myself and didn't lift the thick layer of confusion that covered my own real motives. I didn't know *how* to lift it and I probably wouldn't have known how to understand what it hid. MDA's net – Tom's net – was silky indeed, so silky that by the time I realized how tangled up I was, it was a tough job getting unsnared.

If only I could see that year as one long party with no lasting consequences. But part of untangling the net is admitting that it wasn't. That I came away with scars and maybe others did too. And I was responsible for them.

I used to walk into labs at the local universities and steal the chemical we needed. It was ridiculously easy to wander in, find the right room, locate the precise vial and walk out with it. If anyone stopped me, I knew how to pretend I had legitimate business there. "I'm looking for my father," I said. My father the professor, sure. No one ever doubted my story.

I'm looking for my father. Didn't those words just leap to my lips whenever an excuse was necessary.

I turned 16 that winter. I stopped going to school and didn't go home either and there was nothing anyone could do about it. My mother tried telling the cops I had run away, but they said if I left voluntarily, and if she knew where I was, they couldn't help her.

She did know where I was. One of my friends had told her soon after I moved in with Tom, and she tracked me down and called me there.

"I'm happier here," I told her.

"Is this the way you're going to kill me?" she asked. We spoke to each other through accusations. Her question was loaded with things I didn't want to look at too closely. Kill her by worrying her to death? By bringing more shame on the family? Kill her the way I hadn't killed her that day with the gun?

"He must be queer," she said about Tom. "Why else would he have a young boy at his house?" What I heard was *no one would ever want to do anything for you.* And when she threatened to turn us in to the cops, what I heard was *I won't let you have even this.* All the years she'd complained that I cost too much to feed and now I was on my own, making more money than she'd ever seen. I was finally succeeding at something and she wanted to take it away.

A warped way to look at it? Maybe so. Here's a mother whose son runs away, lives with a known drug dealer, and she can't do anything about it. Wouldn't any mother worry? Can't you see past all the anger and recognize a mother's fears?

What I want to know is, if she was all that worried, why didn't she come get me? When you're caught in a net and drowning, sometimes you even fight your rescuers. I needed someone who would reach in and grab me anyway.

Here's how I got out. When Tom first took me down to the lab where he synthesized the drug, he showed me how to adjust the pH and told me it should always be at 7.5. What he didn't say was *you could die if you screw this up.* Sometimes I wonder whether it would have made any difference if he had, since I was so hell-bent on pushing myself to the limit, always challenging life to convince me it was worth the trouble. After a while I got careless and accepted a pH anywhere near 7.5.

One day I sneaked down to the lab by myself. I'd been on a run, taking drugs just about constantly for a couple of days, and I mixed the dose quickly. A few hours later I started to feel strange enough to say something to Tom. "I feel weird," I admitted. "My back hurts." I didn't tell him my legs were starting to feel heavy too. I waited to see what he'd say, hoping he'd come up with a simple explanation.

"Maybe you strained something," he suggested, and he offered to take me to his chiropractor. I went along with it. As long as I didn't tell Tom what I'd done, maybe nothing serious would happen. But the pain only got worse and I kept popping reds and washing them down with Jack Daniel's to make it go away.

Later in the day a few of us got in the car and headed over to a friend's house. By this time my legs actually felt cold when I touched them, but I kept quiet. And then when I tried to get out of the car, my legs wouldn't hold me. I fell down and lay there in the driveway trying to figure out what was going on. "It must be the reds," someone said, but I knew it wasn't. I felt wide awake; I just couldn't get up.

I managed to get into the house by crawling along the ground. Inside, we sat around for a while trying to pretend nothing was wrong, but it was Tom who finally said, "We've got to take you to the hospital." By the time we pulled up to the emergency room I had stopped telling myself everything was fine. I was flat-out terrified, and I couldn't walk at all. They had to come out to the car and lift me into a wheelchair.

Tom said if they asked what I'd taken I should tell them, but I swore I wouldn't. I was going to hold onto that secret like a soldier in an enemy camp. We both knew it would be dangerous for Tom to come in with me, so I went in alone and tried to look like a nice kid with mysterious symptoms.

They did every test they could think of. Finally the doctor looked me in the eye and admitted, "We don't know what's wrong. Do you do drugs?"

"No, I don't." I tried to sound like the idea was ridiculous. He headed for the door and I figured I'd fooled him. And then with his hand on the knob he suddenly stopped and turned back to me, his eyes fierce.

"Listen, you fool," he yelled, "you've got to tell me what you're on or you're going to die!"

I told him. Every last chemical name.

After that I was in their hands. The spinal tap, an agony like nothing I'd ever known, the operating room, the diagnosis of acute amphetamine poisoning, the eventual gangrene in my right leg and the excision of bits of muscle and bone. Thirty days in the hospital, their round-the-clock care laced with disgust (or was it sorrow) at what drugs were doing to kids who ended up in emergency rooms.

At some point during that first day, they asked for the name of my parent or guardian. I tried to stall. Near as I was to drowning in the pain and fear, I was still hoping I wouldn't have to call my mother and say I needed her. But eventually I told them that, too. I gave them the phone number and soon she was standing over my bed, shaking her head, saying, "Lord have mercy, what have you done to yourself?"

I would have done anything to avoid looking into her eyes and seeing that question there.

Tom stayed away from the hospital. He was in his own trouble by then and didn't need mine. Just before I met him, Tom had been arrested for possession and distribution. In those days, there was an 18-month period between a drug's being discovered and its being declared illegal. MDA was new enough to be hovering in that waiting period, and Tom was awaiting trial the whole time I lived with him. The trial date came soon after I got out of the hospital, and Tom knew he was going to be convicted. That day, when the court recessed for lunch, he just took off. Jumped into his car and headed for California.

He wasn't alone. He had a kid with him, a kid who might have done some serious thinking while he lay in that hospital bed, might have listened when his mother said "You're going to have to come home, go back to school, stop all this craziness." Might have, but didn't. Going home and admitting my mother was right about anything felt like too big a surrender. OK, the fact is I did try it for a couple of weeks – went back home with my leg still in bandages – but it all felt the same, horribly the same, and in the end the wild promise of Tom's next adventure seemed the better deal.

We were a pair of fugitives on the open road and it was strangely exhilarating and strangely comforting too, like being on vacation with Dad. A crazy analogy, but this kid took satisfaction where he could find or invent it. And I believed my real father was in California, so I thought we were headed to my promised land.

Tom's plan was to go to Lake Tahoe, where he was going to hook up with a guy who would help us start up a new MDA lab. We should have been scared, should have known there was no way this could end well, but we covered our tracks and threw people off the scent by zigzagging north and then south instead of heading west in a straight line. Then when we finally got to the coast, the guy we were meeting turned out to be all talk; there was nothing there for us. So we turned around and drove back east, this time to New Orleans: Tom's plan B. Another guy he knew, another hopeful prospect, but by this time the shine of the whole thing was growing dull for me. Everyone we met seemed full of bullshit and empty promises. I started to think I was burdening Tom more than help- ing him, though he denied this whenever I said it. I started to think I did- n't want to be there when he got caught.

So I went home. I actually, finally, gave up and called my mother. I didn't say where I was or where we'd been, but I told her I would come home and get some help.

Tom did get caught and go to jail; I did come home and go to a res- idential treatment center at my mother's urging. But even that didn't bring me back for good. I had to go a lot farther away before I was ready to even think about coming back for real. I look back on those years and see a lot of missed chances, a lot of places where I could have changed course and didn't. But there's one thing I try to keep in mind. As furi- ously destructive as I was, when that doctor demanded the name of the poison, I told him. When it came right down to it I didn't clutch my fist as tightly around the secret as I'd thought I would. I chose to tell him; I chose to save myself. Today when things seem impossibly dark, it helps to remember that even then I chose to live.

"Sit down and don't fucking move." I sit in the chair in the hallway of the house, waiting to see what will happen. A big Black guy comes out, tells me his name is Bruce and he's the director of this place, looks at me and says, "Do you want to change?"

"Of course," I tell him. "Why do you think I'm here?"

He comes right up to me, stands close to the chair, tells me he's not cutting me any slack just because I'm young. "I'm gonna be on your ass the whole time," he says. "Because I care."

Because he *cares?* I can smell my sweat and his, and I want to look away from him and rest my eyes on the clean waxed floor, the black and white squares that have none of Bruce's heat and urgency in them. But the way he's staring down at me, I can't look away until he disappears into the next room and leaves me sitting there. I sit and sit until I hurt from sitting so long, and I keep expecting someone to come and do something but hours pass and even though people come and go, no one says anything to me. Only when I start to nod off does someone yell, "Sit the fuck up! Wake the fuck up and save your life!"

It was just like the doctor at the hospital, and I was almost as scared and disoriented as I'd been then. *If you keep this up, you're going to die!* the doctor had yelled when I finally told him what drugs I was on. He'd backed me into a corner and made me admit I wanted to live enough to let him help me. Now here was Bruce, director and former dope fiend, shoving me into the same corner.

My mother had found this place, a residential therapeutic drug treatment center. I'd fought everything she wanted me to do for so long, but now I was about as ready as I was going to get. I meant it when I told Bruce I wanted to change.

There were 25 of us, male and female, crammed into the rooms of this house, sleeping on bunk beds. I was the youngest one there. The primal therapy approach they believed in meant they tried to rip you apart before they put you back together again. After leaving me to sit for hours in the front hallway, they finally told me to come upstairs. They had to carry me and the chair, that's how weak I was by then. Everyone was there in the room at the top of the stairs, all the residents and counselors and Bruce too. Together they made a heat so suffocating I thought I couldn't breathe, and they told me to put the chair down and sit in it and tell them about myself. *You're a trifling fool drug addict* they yelled back at me, their knowing glances saying to each other, *we're going to break this little prick.*

But wasn't I *already* broken? Hadn't I already surrendered and surrendered?

"What do you want?" someone called from across the room to me in my chair.

"I want help."

"Then *ask* for it!"

I did. Over and over, with tears now. And in that tidal wave of frustration and hope and misery and shame for all the mistakes these past few years had been full of, there was a part of me that wanted to cry out, Goddammit, look what I've been doing since I was 12. Haven't I've *been* asking?

"Welcome to our family," they said when the brutal intake process was over, an idea that was either crazy or tempting or both. Being in their family meant talking about your feelings. In the encounter groups they had a couple of times a week, they asked it over and over: what are you feeling, what are you feeling, what are you —

If I didn't answer immediately, they got right in there and told me. They told me how I felt until I figured maybe they were right. I learned how to say "I feel hurt" with just the right amount of sincerity and surprise.

Yeah, I learned how to fake it. I learned how to say the kinds of things that impressed them. I faked it because it was easier, because I wanted them to like me, because I thought maybe I'd eventually come to feel it for real. So maybe I was exactly the lying cheating fool they said I was. And I used this acting ability later on, when I was long gone from there, doing worse things than I'd ever done but wanting people to believe I was a sensitive, trustworthy guy.

Faking didn't help anyone. But the fact is I didn't know how to do anything else.

That's it. The trouble was I really didn't know the answer to their question. Maybe the realest thing for me in that place was the instant of panicked silence when they asked me how I felt. The silence that could have shown me I had no words, couldn't truly have named the sensations of my own body or mind or heart. Maybe that was where we all should have started: not with easy words but with the terror of not knowing. Like the soldier on the battlefield who hears the medic asking "Does this hurt?" and realizes he can't even feel the guy's hand on his body, can't tell what hurts or doesn't, doesn't even know he's being touched.

What they were doing wasn't really working, but it's not as if I had any better ideas. I could barely even say "I'm hurt" and mean it – I sure as hell didn't have any idea where the sore was. Maybe I thought they were going to find out for me. Maybe I thought all their questions would eventually peel back the layers, unwrap all the bandages, so we could see the real wounds at last.

I stayed for over a year, and I did manage to be sober the whole time. Of course it felt strange at first, after being high all day every day for so long. I missed the comfort, missed how lit-up and neon everything seemed on MDA. But if I was going to be sober it was easier to do it here, 90 miles away from home, surrounded by all these people who were sober too. I was always trying to find some mirror to see myself in. If it wasn't going to be Kenny and Lane and their heroin, if it wasn't going to be MDA, maybe it could be these people here. Even if I was faking so much of it, if I could stay sober the way they were, maybe everything would be OK. I was doing what I was supposed to do. I'd get out, get my GED, maybe even go to college like my brother.

Sometimes I had contempt for them when they couldn't see through me, but mostly I thought they meant what they said and knew what they were doing. I might be faking but at least they were real.

Until the night I came downstairs and found a couple screwing in the bathroom and a bunch of house members outside drinking. There it was – they were hypocrites too. Everybody was. They violated their own rules – rules I had followed for a whole year and believed they were fol-lowing too.

I was the bigger fool, thinking *anybody* was for real. Kid, you learned the fucking lesson when you were 12 and you shouldn't have forgotten it: you *know* what happens if you trust anyone. You know it.

This was it, then – the only thing that kept proving true time and time again.

I left, same as I did before, believing I was cutting everything loose. Won't get fooled again. That's what I told myself, but even as I was say-ing it I was jumping right into something else that I thought would make the difference. I'd left my mother's for the promised haven of MDA and Uncle Tom, and I left the rehab house for what looked like true love – a beautiful woman who had been waiting for me to get out, a woman who would take me higher, and then finally lower, than I'd been yet. I didn't know when I left the group home that I hadn't learned it all yet. Before I completely and utterly gave up, I still had one more round to play.

Lisa was her name, and she was beautiful. So beautiful I thought I could grab onto her and be transported. She looked like Rita Coolidge, which made me think I could be Kris Kristofferson, the country boy saved by a city girl. Lisa's older sister Karen had been at the rehab house with me. "You're cute," she told me. "I should fix you up with my sister." It seemed like Karen was offering me something, and for all I knew, this cure was as likely to work as anything else. By the time Lisa came to visit her sister I was already half in love with the idea of her, and when I saw her I was convinced she could be my magic. We talked that day, wrote letters afterward, had one night in a motel when I got a pass for an overnight leave, and I was sure this was the love I'd been waiting for.

How seductive the promise of rescue is — so seductive you can miss the fact that no one actually promised you anything. It was only your own need all along, the need you've been living with for years, but since no one ever told you *how* to live with it, you've just been filling it with drugs, keeping yourself so doped up you don't even know what you're missing. So you can get to be 17 and believe you're a man in love with a woman, when the truth is you hardly even know what that means.

The night I discovered the rehab house was a sham and all the people in it were liars, I called Lisa as if she were the only true thing left in the world, and told her I had to get out of there. She came and got me, and we spent the night at her mother's house, in her room that still looked like a little girl's bedroom, with flowered wallpaper and the two of us crammed into her single bed. I was so happy to be with her that I didn't care, and I figured I'd done the right thing. I'd start a new life with Lisa. I'd even stay clean, no drugs, just let love carry me.

We moved out of her mother's house and into our own place. I got a job at a rental car company and felt like I was doing things right for once in my life. Sure, my mother hassled me about it: "What are you doing with her, why don't you come home and get your GED, why don't you go to college like Joe?" But I figured my mother was never going to be happy no matter what I did. And meanwhile I was working a regular job, bringing home some honest money, living with this beautiful older woman.

My mother asked what I was doing with Lisa, but to me that answer was obvious. The mystery was what she was doing with me. I could see she wanted to be with me — she came and got me the minute I called her, and she never argued when I suggested we get a place together. But I couldn't have told you why she wanted me. What did I have that some other guy couldn't give her just as well or better? I was dizzy with my luck but always a little on edge. Always waiting for the morning I'd wake up and discover she had changed her mind.

In the sweet radiance of those early days with Lisa, it was easy to stay off drugs. Even if I hadn't really gotten to the roots of anything during my months at the rehab house, I *had* gotten the drugs out of my system. And somehow I didn't quite want to throw that all away when I left.

But it didn't last, none of it did. Lisa drank beer and did bongs and soon enough I slid back into doing them with her. Later, when things started to go bad between us and I was spending my days getting back at her in one way or another, I hung around with enough people who had drug connections that I got sucked in. All the way back in.

I could feel it when Lisa started cooling off toward me. She wasn't so happy to see me anymore, and she wasn't so happy with the jobs I was working either. It seemed like I never made enough money for her — for the clothes she wanted to buy, for the idea she had of a good life. There I was, really still a kid but thrown suddenly into responsible manhood. I was trying to do the right thing and support her, hiding the fact that I hardly knew what I was doing and deep down I'd been hoping she would take care of *me*. It was easy, too easy, to turn to robberies again. When I got scared of not being able to give her what she wanted, I grabbed at the quickest solution I knew.

Sex seemed like another quick solution. I thought as long as we had that together, we'd be OK. But then she pulled back there too. She started coming to bed in the thickest nightgowns possible — uglying herself up, I called it. When she got into bed like that and turned her back to me, I knew I was losing her.

I was running and running and it was impossible. I couldn't stop running and I couldn't catch up to her and keep her either.

I can't bear wanting. I can't bear the way it scoops me out, hollows me, until I am nothing but desire and need and I already *know* what that gets you: nothing. Exactly nothing. Or less than nothing, because it takes and takes until you are less than you were before. Why do I stand here wanting her when she doesn't want me back? I look at her and it's like looking into an empty mirror, no face looking back at you. So why do I keep on looking? Why don't I know to turn away?

I turned away from my mother because her hard eyes never softened into warmth and I was sick of looking into them and hoping. So why did I start hoping all over again with Lisa? Why did I think she could give me back to myself? If only I could be all the way cold. Why can't I take this warm beating thing inside of me, this open hopeful this fucking *desperate* part of me and tear it out? If you wait for mercy you could wait forever. And it doesn't matter how much you beg or how deserving you are. When the well is dry it's dry.

The colder Lisa is to me the more disembodied I feel. After a while I can't feel her anymore and I can't even feel *me*. In bed with other women, I try to bring myself back, try like someone working to revive the dead: slap the face, shake the body, come on, come on, are you awake, can you feel this? And for a while I do feel it, or feel the power anyway. Look what I am, Lisa, Mom, everyone: I am someone women want, and I can have whatever I think of, but I don't *need* anything.

I storm into a jewelry store and demand what's behind the counter. The guy starts to reach for his gun and I can't believe he would even try. Doesn't he know who he's messing with? Doesn't he know there's nothing he can do about it? If he thinks there's a way out of this, he better learn fast. There is never a way out. And sure enough he takes his hand away and gives in, gives up, gives me what I want. Tearing out of there I feel it, the same thrill I felt at 13 only way, way more.

When you're that disembodied, this is what it takes just to feel your own heart in your chest. This is what it takes just to believe you're alive.

But nothing ever worked for long, and nothing was ever enough for her. Or for me. What I wanted from Lisa was more than any one person should want from another: salvation, restoration of myself, a way out of the cage I lived in. There was probably no way for it to end well. How does it ever end, the story of a beautiful woman and the desperate guy who believes he loves her more than anything else in the world?

She's going out to see a girlfriend and I won't sit home alone, so I ask her to drop me off at Diamond Jim's downtown. I'm drinking my favorite wine on the way, holding the bottle close. Something about the way she looks at me as she lets me out of the car tells me she's thinking about me even less tonight than she does any other night. I tell her I love her and she doesn't say anything, so – as if my spite still matters to her – I say, "I'll have picked up and gotten rid of three women by the time you get back." She shrugs and takes off.

Inside, I see women I know and I make good on my promise to Lisa: I flirt with everyone and bring them close, so close to believing I'm about to go home with them, but each time at the last minute I change my mind. I'm talking to one of them when Lisa comes to get me, and I shrug and say, "Sorry, the woman I love just walked in the door." I smile as if any woman would understand how helpless love leaves you, but this woman at the bar's got no sympathy for me. She's duped and furious and I just manage to duck before the beer she hurls at me splashes on the table. I head over to Lisa, hoping she sees the trouble I got into for her. All she says is, "What's *with* you?" and heads out to the car.

We're driving home. Lisa's friend Tricia is in the back seat. No one's talking and I don't know what it is but there's something strange in the air. I keep looking back and forth between them and suddenly I have an idea, a guess so terrible I blurt it out before I even think about it:

"You're sucking her cunt, aren't you?"

They don't say anything, and their silence is the answer.

Jesus, it's *true!* I thought I was just crazy and now it turns out I'm right. Righter than I ever wanted to be. I worried she was out with other guys and instead it's been this girl, this girl looking so scared in the back seat, and Lisa doesn't need me now and she never did and I can't stand to look at her and think about it.

We're at a stoplight and I open the car door, grab the empty wine bottle from under the seat, and hurl it on the road. So inevitable, that smash and shatter. Like there is no other choice. I tell Lisa *I'm going to cut your face.* I am going to, I'm ready, I can see her pressed up against the seat trying to get away from me, and I've got the broken neck of the bottle in my hand, waiting, and then I can't do it. I can't cut that face that was always so beautiful to me, so beautiful it's like a knife twisting in my heart. No, I can't hurt her there – what I need to do is hurt her where *I'm* hurting.

I start hitting her and Tricia is in the middle trying to stop me and then the cops roll up next to us and look in the window, but when they figure out it's a domestic dispute they don't want to mess with it. I'm yelling *drive the car* and she drives, and it's over it's over it's dead there is nothing left. We're in front of the house and I leap out of the car, my fists flying everywhere, beating on the hood, dragging Lisa out, and then I'm running inside, crashing through the screen door, and the heat of the betrayal is flaming all around my ankles. I can't outrun it. I can hardly see anything in front of me as I race to find the gun, and gripping it in my hands I think *I should just shoot myself.* Just end the fucking misery because it's never going to get any better. But she's the one! She's the one doing this to me, she's the one bringing all this pain, and it flips around in my mind so I'm sure the thing to do is to get rid of her, not me.

All at once I'm outside in the yard with the pines shielding us from the neighbors and I'm shooting at her in a wild despair, like trying to save my own life but knowing it's hopeless. The bullets keep missing her and I run back inside for more. And here is Lisa's sister Karen, blocking my path and asking me calmly what I'm doing. "What do you want to do that for?" she says after I tell her. "She's not worth a day in prison."

Karen's trying to get me to see past this moment but all I can think is *without Lisa I feel like I'm in prison anyway.* There's no way out no matter how you look at it. I'm boxed in, I have to give up, and somehow Karen's steady gaze is reaching me so when she says "give me the gun" I do give it to her.

On the couch now I'm crying, the tears bleeding out of me, because now I know I have nothing left. This was my last chance and it's over; there will never be a way out for me. And what I wish, what I just wish, that she could have been different, that I could have been different, that I could have found a way to live in the world of other people and be loved – this is not a wish I will get.

It wasn't just luck that made those bullets miss. It must have been at least partly my own desperate ambivalence that saved Lisa, because I didn't really want to kill her. But what I did want seemed impossible – and the agony of that was too much for me. I just plain didn't have what it took to bear it. And Lisa was the one who paid.

Well, Karen paid too. I'll never know if she meant it when she said her sister wasn't worth it, or if she was only saying whatever would get me to put the gun down. But either way, it's got to have been a terrible night for her.

Shooting at Lisa was about giving up and refusing to admit it was time to give up, all in a crazy mix. Afterwards it was as if something I'd been struggling with since I was 12 finally just curled up and died. I stopped even trying to be good, or whole, or connected to the world around me. I was 19 when I left her and the next two years were a race against time: how long can I live like this, like I don't care at all, before something happens to crash it all to a stop?

The funny thing is, even when you think you've given up all the way, there's something inside that hangs on. Even when I thought I'd given up hope, I hadn't, but I'd disguised it so thoroughly I couldn't recognize it anymore. You *can't* recognize your own longing when it seems so monstrous and impossible, when the very idea of hoping is like a crazy hunger you're never going to fill. The desire for love, for peace, for comfort, for my father, for a return from exile – by the time I was 20 and running on my own, all this was so overwhelming, the only name I could give it was rage.

So I was angry and gone, trying to fool myself and everyone else. I was good at it too. When I talked to someone who lived in the legitimate world, I could fabricate a believable story about why I was traveling around so footloose and free. I'm taking time off before college, I'd say. My father's given me some money so I can travel for a while.

No accident that a generous father regularly appeared in these cover stories. I built myself a make-believe castle of protection and care and tried to convince people I really lived there. I thought they were so gullible for believing what I told them. They were, but so was I. I kept believing I could numb myself, distract myself, pretend a decent father was watching over me so I wouldn't have to hear the voice continually accusing, pleading with him in my mind: *why weren't you there? Why the fuck weren't you there when I needed you?*

Yeah, I hadn't gotten over it. How different was I really from the boy who kept asking, "Did my father call?" When my mother told me he hadn't, she wasn't sorry. All those times she yelled "You're just like your father," all those times I threw it back in her face, and inside me was that secret: I wanted him. Wanted him anyway, bad as he was. And so if I couldn't bring him back, maybe becoming like him could bind us together in some mysterious way I didn't even fully understand. *You're just like your father.* The thing is, I knew it. I knew he had made me just as surely as she had. Even if the father part of me was the part she hated, I couldn't disgorge it, not even to please her.

So now I let her be the one to sit and wait for a phone call that never came. After practicing leaving home so many times, leaving for good was easy. I was just gone, and not like other sons who had someplace to go *to* and whose mothers could brag to their friends about where they were. I was everywhere and nowhere: on the Florida beaches, in New York clubs, on the Chicago streets, wherever life masqueraded as an easy carnival I could hide myself in.

Here it is, any night and every night during the continuous party of the late '70s. Donna Summer is singing *Love to Love You Baby*, and the slow heat of it, the way she seems to caress the words with her voice, reminds me of heavy summer days in North Carolina, the air thick with honeysuckle and promises that come easily to the lips. I could walk up to any woman right now and sing along to those lyrics and she'd believe me. In my white pants and leather belt and loafers, my jacket open and the tie loosened just the right amount, I look like I can make anything happen. And I can. I'll go up to the woman who's sitting alone at the end of the bar, pretending she doesn't care. I'll tell her exactly what she wants to hear, my words as persuasive as any song's. I'll show her she does care, and then I'll walk away.

It was almost too easy. I'd look at them and think, *you fool.* You believe in fairytales. Someone tells you he loves you, tells you he'll call, and you believe it because you want it so badly. Don't you know it ain't gonna happen? Don't you know what I know?

I loved this game, got high on repeating it over and over. But sometimes, afterwards, the terrible emptiness of it would blow over me and I would shiver, even in the hot shower, even in the high-priced hotel room. Those mornings, all the colors of the night before would be bleached out and I'd be left staring at the blank wall across the room, the wall of a place where no one lives.

I stood on a dock by the Florida ocean helping a guy unload duffel bags of drugs and making sure no one stole them. The sun burned the scene into my mind like a photograph, and suddenly I heard my mother's voice, years before, telling me my father was a big-time drug dealer in California. She didn't know it for sure; it was just something she'd heard. But true or not, it was what we had of him, and standing on the dock that day it hit me: I've done it. I've become like him. I'm everything she said he was – I've got the drugs, the women, and even, in my own way, the gambling.

He took me to the dog races that last summer we spent together. It wasn't for my benefit; he went where he needed to go and brought me along. Before he went into the stadium, he asked me to pick some numbers, and I picked 1 and 2. I can still see those numbers chalked on the inside of my mind, can still feel how much I wanted to do this for him. I waited behind the bleachers and the chain-link fence. I couldn't see the dogs but I could hear the people cheering and smell the anticipation, and I could see the scoreboard clearly enough to see that we'd won, even before he came out to tell me.

We won, Dad, remember? And guess what: now I'm a bigger gambler than you were. I can lie in a ditch, trembling, while the cops race past me and never know what I have. I'm better than you were at all your games. What would you think if you could see me now?

He didn't realize that all those years, someone was watching him. He didn't realize that when he disappeared, he left something behind: a space I'd have to fill, inside me and out, a silhouette of a missing man I'd have to step into and try to match. Standing on that dock a continent away from him, I knew I'd done it. I felt it all the way through my body, the grown-up body he'd never seen. Everything my mother accused him of was true of me.

And did it bring him any closer?

You never know, ahead of time, which are the days that will change your life. A bar owner I knew in Florida told me about a possible score in Boston. An opportunity to rob someone, if you were so inclined, and he knew I was. He'd heard about it from an 18-year-old gay hustler named Steve. Steve said he'd been up in Boston with an antique dealer he'd hustled and had seen a huge pile of money right there in the house. $300,000, the bar owner told me. I could feel the number slam against me, the idea of it, the possibility that so much money would finally give me what I'd been looking for. *I'm interested*, I told him, and he introduced me to Steve. Even though I was only 21 myself, Steve seemed like a kid to me, but I knew he was necessary. With him along we wouldn't have to break into the house - we could walk up to the door like ordinary visitors. But we needed a third partner too, someone meaner and more experienced than Steve, someone ready to be as ruthless as I was. Within 24 hours, I'd put everything together. I found Mitch, our third man. Collected everything we needed. Got in the car and headed up to Boston.

You know the charge was attempted murder, so you already know that no one is going to die in this story. When you hear the facts, you might think we tried to kill the victims only to save our own skins, because we'd gone in without masks and the robbery had gotten out of control. But the truth is they were doomed from the start. These innocent people were as easy to target as anyone. Easier, in fact, because I knew at least one of them was gay and that let me see him as less than human. I didn't know enough to analyze that feeling or try to do anything else about it. Rage was in charge, but it was a strange, disguised master: it drove me on but shielded its face from me so I could never see its source. I was headed up to Boston and all I knew was that I wanted the money and would do anything to get it. This is my real accounting, and it may not help anyone to hear it. But the truth is what I've got, finally, and it seems right to offer it.

We walk up to the house, the three of us. Sure enough, the antique dealer invites us in. If he's surprised that this kid he met in Florida has come back to visit him and brought two friends, he doesn't show it. We introduce ourselves, make small talk, let him believe this is what it appears. Let him settle comfortably into his innocence for a while. I actually savor this, knowing exactly how it will feel when we rip that comfort out from under him. He sits at his desk at the far end of the room, and while his hands are out in full view in front of him, I make my move, cross the room in an instant and put the pistol between his eyes.

"Don't move!" I watch as the shock of it invades him. "We're here to rob you. Don't do anything stupid." Don't try to reach for any kind of alarm or panic button, is what I mean. Don't even think of trying to save yourself.

Across the room I see a younger man, could be this guy's lover, standing in equal shock as Mitch points his gun at him. He starts to move, ignoring my command to freeze.

"That's a very stupid thing you're doing," I say, low and mean. Doesn't he know there's nothing to do but surrender? I've seen this before: at the beginning, people still believe they have a chance. I wait it out, and the inevitable collapse always comes. It's something you can almost *see*, how they give in to the helplessness. They recognize that I have all the power and they have none of it.

"Where's the $300,000?" I demand of the antique dealer.

"It's gone."

"Gone where?"

"At the bank. I'll give it to you – I'll give you everything I have in the bank."

Any idea that we've made a mistake here gets overshadowed by the seductive appeal of that money in the bank. He's scared, I know it, and even though this isn't as easy as we'd hoped, he's still mine. He'll do anything to keep from being hurt. *What a fool you are*, I think as I look into his suntanned face, his carefully combed hair. You still think if you go along with this you'll be safe. You still believe you have that much control. Of course, that's what we *tell* you. We say, "Just do what I say and everything will be fine," but our secret is that you've already lost. Nothing is fine and there's nothing you can do to make it be fine. When I let you in on this secret, when I surprise you later by hurting you even though you've done everything I've ordered you to do, I'll say "I lied" and I'll relish the look of final surrender in your eyes.

Meanwhile, we're the ones who keep having to adjust to surprises, but I'm still sure I can cope with every one. There's a plumber in the house with these two men, a man who is so completely in the wrong place at the wrong time that I could almost feel sorry for him, but I don't, not then. I take him and the lover upstairs to the attic and tie them up with rope and an extension cord I find there. I tell Steve to watch them while Mitch and I escort the antique dealer to the bank.

"If they do anything, kill them," I order Steve. I make sure they hear me say it. It's clear what we have to do. We can't leave without getting anything. We have to go through with this trip to the bank. I turn to leave the attic and I see a safe, but it's only got pennies inside. In a fury I kick it down the stairs. I'm getting myself as outraged as I need to be for what we have to do.

We get in the car – me at the wheel, the antique dealer next to me, and Mitch at his back keeping the pistol pointed at him. I coach him about what to say when we get to the bank. It's an acting lesson, quick and fierce: say we're your nephews and you need to show us something in your safe deposit box. If you try to signal to anyone, I'll see and I'll pull this trigger.

We're in the bank, standing at the safe, when a cop comes by and leans over, right next to me, so close I can see the pores of his face. His hand is at his waist, and I'm sure he knows what's going on and is reaching for his gun. My own hand is inside the pocket of my sweatshirt, gripping the pistol. My finger is tight on the trigger and I come within a second of pulling it when I realize I don't have to. The cop doesn't know. He's only reaching for a key on his belt, a key he's going to use to record his daily rounds the way night watchmen in factories do. I'm right in the middle of a robbery and a hair's breadth away from raising the stakes, but just as I skid up to the moment, I see my mistake and relax my finger. The adrenaline floods through me and I turn back to the antique dealer, who is playing his part well.

We get back into the car. We've pulled off the charade, but even though he's cleaned out the safe, there's only $7,000.

"We're still a little short," I say angrily. "I know there's at least $300,000 somewhere."

"Actually, there was $500,000 here yesterday, but you missed it by a day."

Is he really saying this? I can't believe he's taunting me, mocking my bad luck. How can he mock me when he's the fool? He's the one with the pistol at his back, doing whatever we tell him to do. I have the power here, and I can't stand watching him act even for a minute as if that's not true. I'm even readier to punish him than I was before.

Back at the house, Steve's still watching the other two men, but nervously. He's tired of being alone with them and scared because they've managed to loosen themselves a little. I tell him the score isn't what we thought. There's only $7,000. The three of us go into a huddle, and I tell Steve he's the one who brought us here, so he should go first and do what we know has to be done. He balks, though, still a scared kid. Now I'm furious with him, too. Of course we can't just go and leave these guys; we've been with them without any masks for close to an hour. I don't understand why Steve won't follow through, why he isn't angry enough to *want* to follow through.

"Fuck it, I'll do it myself," I tell him in disgust. I know I have to start with the lover, because he's the youngest and strongest, so I put a plastic bag over his head and start trying to strangle him. He takes it, barely makes any noise, and I realize this isn't satisfying me. I want to see him really squirm, so I take out my knife. But just as the knife reaches him, just as I see the blood, the plumber makes a desperate dive for his life and lurches down the stairs. His legs are still tied together, and since he's tethered to the lover, too, he jerks him after him, which pulls me along too until we've all tumbled down the stairs together. On the second floor I see Steve standing paralyzed. He can't think what to do but he's trying desperately to look helpful. Mitch is down on the first floor watching the antique dealer, but as he turns his head in surprise at the sound of the three of us thudding down the stairs, the dealer escapes, running for the side door of the house. Instantly Mitch is shooting at him; I hear the shots even before I reach the first floor. But the dealer gets outside, and before I know it the other two have untangled themselves and are running too. The plumber runs in one direction. The lover, still bleeding, runs in another. I shoot at them, watching as they disappear over the seawall by the beach, and out of the corner of my eye I see a woman, down the street, standing frozen at her mailbox. Something about it stays in my mind: how strange she looks juxtaposed into this scene, like someone who has wandered into the wrong painting.

There we are in broad daylight on the main drag of this town, and we have to face the fact that this robbery is completely blown. The three of us go back into the house, gambling with the few minutes we'll have before the cops and ambulances arrive. We race around spraying Endust on the doorknobs, snatching up the ashtrays with our cigarette butts in them, stuffing everything into a duffel bag. In one final moment of reckless arrogance, I grab a case of beer that's sitting there, hoist it onto my shoulder, and stride across the street to our car as though I'm not the man anyone's looking for. The sirens are screaming from every direction and I'm at the car but I can't find the keys. My hand is actually shaking, and for that one moment I let myself feel the panic, but then I force myself to focus. I get the keys, we all barrel into the car, and I crank it up and tear out just as a cop car is coming down the street the other way. He careens around the curb, just missing us, rushing to the scene of the crime as the perpetrators speed past him, gone.

Hours later, Mitch, Steve, and I are standing in a rock quarry in New Jersey. We've gotten away. I'm ready to shoot Steve for his uselessness, his incompetence, but Mitch talks me out of it and we put Steve on a bus for home. I'm still so sure it's Steve's fault that the money wasn't there, that the men got away. It doesn't occur to me that maybe it was my fault for bringing an inexperienced kid into this situation. It doesn't occur to me that sometimes things just go wrong. It doesn't occur to me that no matter who else I blame, I stood over those men and almost took their lives.

Mitch and I lay low in New Jersey for a couple of weeks. We're a little antsy, worrying that we left things open in Boston, but we put it out of our minds by biding our time and partying night after night. One night in a bar with Mitch I suddenly get a feeling that it's time to leave. Just one of my feelings, and I tell Mitch I'm out of here, but he says, "Hey man, don't go yet." I let him talk me into staying, but it bothers me. We go back to the motel, and that night I sleep with my gun under my pillow, like I always do. The next morning I wake up hung over and irritated that I didn't leave when I had the instinct to go. I tell Mitch we're leaving today for sure.

In the car, a couple of miles from the motel, the thought hits me like a punch in the stomach: *I left the gun there.* Cursing my stupidity, I double back and hope the maid hasn't gone into the room yet.

I'm driving back down the street toward the motel when I see a cop car coming from the other direction. His brake lights flash, and I know my car's the one he's looking for. "We've been made," I say to Mitch. We're done. I pull up in front of a bar and tell Mitch to save himself, disappear.

Alone now, I start circling around, looking for a big parking lot where I can lose the car and then get away on foot. Panic rises inside me but I fight it, park the car, run through the lot, but the next thing I know I'm surrounded by cops, out of their cars and chasing after me. My feet pound the asphalt, my heart throbs in my throat. Every cell on fire, I feel as if someone threw a switch and made the sky turn black. *It's over it's over it's over.* I hear them yell "Freeze!" They're standing in shooting position, and when I freeze, they throw me on the ground and cuff my hands behind my back, just as pumped up and jittery as I am. They lift me up and throw me into the car, slamming me against the door and then saying "Oh, duck," as an afterthought. I let myself feel the terror now: it's finally happened. Can I bluff it? Is there still any chance? I can't tell.

They deliver me to the cell, and I wait to see what will happen. I don't know how much they know.

Soon enough I discover they know everything. "Massachusetts is on its way," the New Jersey cop tells me ominously.

"What are they coming for?" I ask. I'm fishing for details because I don't know what exactly we left behind in Boston.

"Armed robbery and nearly killing two people," is the reply, and at least I know the men didn't die, the charge won't be murder. The cops have caught Mitch and now they're after me to tell them where Steve is. "Where's your friend?" they keep asking. I don't answer, and it ends up taking them months to find him.

The Massachusetts state police come to drive me back to Boston. There's a strange courteousness about it as we spend those hours in the car together. "Let me know when you're hungry, when you have to go to the bathroom," one tells me. When we stop for food, I order a hamburger and a shake, not yet knowing that these will be the foods I will crave in prison. It's only just beginning to dawn on me that everything I'm doing now, I'm doing for the last time. Or at least for as far into the future as I can see.

The thing I've tried to avoid has finally happened, and I feel ruined, defeated, about to surrender to something I have no idea if I'll even survive. But when I let myself sink back into the knowledge, there's actually relief in it too. It's happened. I don't have to keep looking over my shoulder anymore, waiting for it. And maybe I can stop trying to fit into this world. *I never belonged out there,* something inside me says, and the resignation feels almost like comfort. Maybe prison's where I'm meant to be.

Years later, standing in front of the mirror, I look into my eyes the way I wouldn't look into the eyes of my victims. I try to keep on looking even when what stares back makes me flinch. I see the determination – to tell this story and tell it true, no matter how hard it is. I see the supplication – that maybe something good can come from the telling. I know I can't climb out of this body. Nothing I do, no distance I travel, will let me say these hands aren't mine and I didn't do these things. I still don't know for sure that there can ever be peace or that it's even my right to hope for it. Some days I've stood overlooking the river, staring into the steely gray and thinking, if I jumped, maybe that would restore the balance somehow. Or maybe that's too easy. The harder thing, maybe the better thing, is to go on, even with these hands, these truths. I don't want this to be who I was, I don't want this to be what I did. Remorse is real. It's harder than any day in prison.

I wore black to the courthouse, figuring I might as well look the part. Ninety days in the jail, waiting for the court date, had begun to teach me how things would be. I was already getting used to the rusted toilet, the mesh on the windows so thick it was impossible to see out. I approached this final ritual expecting no surprises. It was all in a day's work for the public defender as he laid it out for me: plead guilty and you'll get 20-30 years, but you'll be on the street sooner than that. In those days you could be eligible for parole after serving two-thirds of the minimum sentence and you could wrap up the sentence completely after serving two-thirds of the maximum. Two-thirds of any of those numbers still seemed like the rest of my life to me, but I had to go along with it. "You've got three people who can positively ID you," the lawyer reminded me. "There's not much else you can do."

My mother, desperate now to save me, wasn't ready to believe this was out of her hands. On the phone she swore she'd get another lawyer, but I told her not to waste her money. A high-priced lawyer she used all her money to hire wouldn't get me out of this, and I was too ashamed to take her help anyway. For two years she'd heard nothing from me. If she'd imagined I was going to school or working a decent job, those illusions were now so completely shattered I couldn't bear to stay on the phone with her. Couldn't stand listening to her trying to make this not be true. *Nothing is fine and there's nothing you can do to make it be fine.* Give up hoping, Mom, because I have. I'll plea out, get the best sentence I can, and be done with it.

The judge seemed larger than life, an imposing God the father with gray hair who stared at me over his half glasses. When the victims testified, I could feel him watching me watch them. I was scanning for scars and nothing was visible. But then the prosecutor asked the young man to show where he was stabbed, and he took off his suit jacket and touched his hand to the place. What is it like to dress up in a suit and stand facing the man who terrorized you and show everyone the place he claimed?

Who had the power now? I looked at them and saw I'd taken something from them. There was a theft and I'd done it, but now I was the one who was caught and it was their fault for not playing their part correctly. After they told their stories, the judge asked each one, "Do you see that person in the room today?" One after the other, they pointed their fingers at me. *You can't get out of this now.* Just as I'd said it to them. No cover, no escape.

The judge watched it all. He could see right through this day to the day months before, when I'd almost killed these men. He could see I wasn't sorry for them then and wasn't now. I took the stand, and he went through the story again, cloaking it in the language of the court:

"And did you enter into a dwelling with intent to commit a felony, to wit: armed robbery and assault with a deadly weapon?"

"Yes."

"Did you enter into the dwelling and therein commit an act which caused injury?"

"Yes," I said again, and again, surrendering each time. The facts crashed over me and I went under each time, owning up to them, but only because I had to. Not because I was ready to think about what they really meant.

I spent the lunch break in an isolated cell off to the side of the bullpen where the other defendants were held. Back again, the dark oak walls of the witness box closing in around me like a phone booth or an upright coffin. I waited to hear the judge's sentence.

He began to read: Home invasion, three counts of armed robbery, three counts of assault with a deadly weapon, two counts of attempted murder. By the time he was finished, I had four concurrent 28-30 year sentences, three 5-10s, also to run concurrently with the other sentences, and two 10-15s, to commence, as 3-year probationary sentences, upon my release from prison. As the numbers piled up around me, all I could think was that the public defender had promised I'd get 20-30 and here I was getting 8 years more. It was another betrayal: I had trusted the lawyer because he was all I had, and it turned out he made a promise he couldn't keep.

The moment the first sentence was announced, court officers appeared like stagehands from the wings to snap the cuffs on me, so I stood cuffed and flanked by these two men as I listened to the judge complete his litany. I was trying to absorb it, to imagine what these numbers would mean. And then the judge paused, and I looked up at him. His eyes seemed to bore right into my body. The official words were finished, but he had something else to say.

"I consider you beyond rehabilitation," he announced, and something split open inside me. He'd seen through to my core and confirmed it: I'm bad, through and through, and there's no point in trying to be anything different. Ten years of wrestling with it, telling myself *you're just evil* and then arguing *no, not all the way,* and now it had come to this: he'd set-tled the question once and for all. I dropped my head and cried, not even trying to hide the tears from him. He knew everything anyway.

When I looked up, he was still staring, fiercely.

"Or maybe not," he said suddenly. "Maybe somewhere down the line, something will change you."

Maybe not? It was too much to take in. The hand that had thrown the shroud of condemnation over my head now lifted it briefly, letting in a thin light of possibility. I had no idea what to believe.

"Go in Godspeed," he concluded. It was the first time I'd heard it, that word meaning "with the grace of God."

I let myself be led from the room, without any grace I could feel. I had no picture of what I was walking toward, no vision of the nightmare that still awaited me or the hope I would eventually find, rough-hewn and surprising, inside those dark hours.

What did you see? You looked at me and you said I was beyond hope and you couldn't even imagine how ready I was to believe you. You grabbed me up by the scruff of the neck and said *this is what you are* and that's what I'd been wanting, someone to take me up and tell me. Someone with a special kind of vision who could see right through me and tell me for sure. And when you said *you're bad, you're all the way bad,* well it made sense that any goodness had been conquered long ago. I was just like my father, possessed of that demon rage that sent him leaving, always trying to escape his own skin. He couldn't live inside it, couldn't wake each day to the things he'd done or failed to do.

And then he was gone when the broken man decided to break me too. The rapist was a judge too. He looked at me and decided what my fate would be, and then the sentence he handed out was perpetual segregation time. He threw me into my own special isolation, saying *This is what you get for even thinking you can be good. This is what you get for wanting someone to look up to.* Like standing under a burning sun with your clothes scorched off and there is no sheltering shade, and your skin burns and scars and you become someone who will never imagine protection again. And won't let anyone else imagine it either.

So you knew that, didn't you, when you said I was beyond rehabilitation? You could see that it was too late for me; I'd spun so far out that there was no possibility of return.

Except there was. You said that too. You changed your mind, just when I thought you had in your wisdom seen the truth and declared it. Maybe not, you said. A loophole, a reprieve, a strange glimmer of possibility that makes me go back even farther in my mind. My dog's rough tongue slathers my face as we tumble together, and I get up and skim oyster shells across the swamp, fingering the craggy disks and smelling the brine in the air, and this is not a boy who is rotten to the core.

Did you see him too that day in the courtroom when you looked at me and saw everything?

What *did* you see? You stamped a crossroads across my mind and sent me away, reeling, to a world I couldn't imagine. Could *you* imagine it? Did you know that your words would reverberate against the walls of my mind, inside all those hollow hours you'd sentenced me to fill? After you said "Beyond hope" and then said "Maybe not," did *you* wonder which one it would be? Does anyone wonder what happens to men after they disappear behind that wall?

What do *I* see? I stare across the cell and there is nothing there. Or there's a picture of a lighthouse that I've taped to the opposite wall. I'm looking up from the floor with swollen eyes after the guards have beaten me almost unconscious and still I'm shouting insults at them. Or I'm staring at a book and forcing myself to understand it. "Which I is *I*?" the poem asks. Instead of giving me an answer you just left the question there, open and haunting, so I had to figure it out myself.

We're taken in a van, our hands cuffed to waist chains at our sides and another chain connecting each man to the one behind him. I watch out the windshield, strain to see through the layer of wire mesh and Plexiglas that separates us from the driver. We're heading to Walpole, the maximum security prison, but only some of us will end up serving our sentences there.

The guy next to me won't stop talking. "I can't believe it, I got 6 to 10 years," he complains. Six to 10? Jesus, my own sentence is three times that. I don't know whether bragging about this will make me seem tough or just stupid, so I keep quiet. Finally he asks me,

"How much time are you doing?"

"28-30," I tell him, just saying it without inflection.

"Whew, you got smoked," he says, shaking his head, and the others laugh. I feel the slap of the public defender's broken promise all over again.

Arriving at Walpole, we're herded through all the gates and doors. I keep stumbling as I try to follow the steps in this strange dance. Finally we're uncuffed and taken to the booking area one at a time. The cop reaches to get my fingerprints, and I start to panic as I feel his hand overtake mine, but I don't pull away.

Next come the photos. Face left, turn right, look over there. Should I smile? No, I keep it serious. This is a picture of a convicted felon.

Supper on a tray, my first prison meal, and the guards tell me I'll be going to the Reception and Diagnostic Center at Concord. The older cons, overhearing this, tell me that's good news. "If you're going to the RDC in Concord," one says, "you'll probably stay there, and that's a better deal than here."

At Concord, the intake counselor runs through a series of questions, getting the information and assessing my grip on reality at the same time. Birthdate, what I'm in for, mother's name and address. I answer everything.

"Is your father living?"

"Yes," I tell her, and my gut clenches because I don't know the answer for sure, couldn't prove it if I had to.

"Address?" she continues.

"I don't know. I haven't seen him since I was 11."

How many men, passing through the RDC, could give their father's address? An intact family was as rare in prison as a college education or inherited wealth. Some guys had never known their fathers. Others had them and lost them, like me. Or had one but got along so badly they missed him as much as if he'd been gone. They grew up piecing together an image of who they believed or hoped or wished he was. They tried to bring him closer by becoming like him, the way I did. Or they spat in the face of his abandonment by becoming what he hated, the way my friend Sean taunted the image of his missing policeman father by becoming the kind of man a policeman hunts. Whatever we'd done about our fathers, that simple question about his name and address made us feel like kids facing a test question we couldn't answer.

That first night at Concord I lay on the top bunk, staring at the ceiling. I'd talked a little with my cellmate but now he was quiet. The only noise was the clanging of the doors. I turned to look out the window, and all I could see besides the wall was a little strip of sky, a patch of grass. *That's as close to all that as I'll get for a while*, I told myself. I was starting to get the idea: it didn't matter any more whether I *wanted* to go home.

"Lenny, can I get a cigarette?" I ask, knowing he'll give me one.

"Sure, kid," he says in the gruff but obliging way he says everything. He hands it to me and grins, showing his gaping mouth, his single tooth. We stand in the yard and watch the other guys go by, see the guard walk past, checking to see if we're doing anything we shouldn't be. Right this minute, we aren't. We're just two guys enjoying a smoke.

I was at Norfolk now, a prison about an hour away from Concord, where there were older guys like Lenny in addition to younger ones like me. Concord was for younger men and after only a couple of months there they said I was "aging out" – I was about to turn 22 – and the administration decided it was time to transfer me to Norfolk, where security was a little tighter, where it felt more like an adult prison, and where it looked like I would stay for a while.

Lenny finishes his cigarette and starts sucking on his tooth contemplatively. He's never in a hurry. After a while he sighs and says aloud, "Well, what can you do?" It doesn't matter what he's referring to. I know he's talking about all of it – us, our lives, the fact that things didn't go the way we planned, that we're standing here in a prison yard and can't go home. What can you do, he always says, shrugging his acceptance of the hand we've been dealt. This is the situation; got to find a way to deal with it.

Lenny actually knew a lot about dealing with it. He'd done time before and as soon as he arrived at Norfolk he got busy settling in, figuring out a plan for making it bearable. I was grateful to have hooked up with him and to take his wordless lessons. Together we stole fruit juice, sugar, rice (for the starch), 5-gallon buckets from the kitchen. We unscrewed a panel in one of the cells; I shimmied up through the crawl space behind it, rope in hand. Crouching among the musty rafters, swatting away the bees, I called down to tell them I was ready. Lenny and his accomplice attached the rope to the bucket and I pulled it up, hand over hand, careful because if it spilled, the smell would fill the tier. *I'll be right down*, I whispered, and they put the panel back and waited. Eight minutes, it took, to cut a hole in the roof of the vent system, hide the bucket there, tie a t-shirt over the top of it so the bugs wouldn't get in, and shimmy back down. Then we all waited, as little as four days during the heat of summer, three times that during the winter months. When the time was right, Lenny would come sauntering up to me, rubbing his hands over his big belly, saying, "I think it's about time for some home brew." He made me laugh just by the way he said it, by the way he could take pleasure in the smallest things. We brought the bucket back to his cell and strained the brew through another t-shirt, wringing it out to get every drop. Word got out that we were ready and other guys would wander in as if by accident, their empty Maxwell House coffee jars in hand. They drank their rations, nodding and saying to each other, "Yeah, I'm buzzed," trying to talk themselves into it.

Lock up a man who's spent years trying to outrun not only the cops but his own scrabbling monsters, who hides from himself so well he hardly remembers he's hiding, and he'll think of pills and even the weakest home brew first, before he thinks of any other way to get through the days. Like Lenny, I got busy as soon as I arrived. I got to work figuring out how to put enough gauze between my eyes and the razor wire, the gates, the walls.

Norfolk was organized into units called houses, with a quad joining them. We lived in single cells. The gate at the end of the tier was locked at night, but during the daytime it was open, and with a pass we could walk out to the yard or to another house. Going onto someone else's tier wasn't allowed, but you could stand in the stairwell and yell for a friend to come down. The whistle blew to wake us up each morning and then to signal mealtimes: 7:00, 11:45, 4:45. Head counts kept track of us as we filed through the cafeteria line; you had to show up for the line even if you didn't want to eat. Guys often tried to sleep the day away and would sleep through the whistle, but a cop would come and wake him if a friend didn't get there first to warn him.

I didn't sleep the day away but I spent a lot of time blurring the edges of it. It was easy to justify. The verdict was in, the door had slammed, and it was easy enough not to feel guilty for wasting my life; I'd already wasted it. In a way, it was as if I'd outlived myself. Getting caught had seemed the worst nightmare, and here I was, beyond it. Just that fact brought a certain lightness and relief: I'm in prison, and this is how it is. And I don't even have to pretend to be a citizen of the world.

Conversations never got too personal, with Lenny or with anyone else. The closest I got to self-reflection was talking with other guys about where we'd gone wrong. But what we meant was *how did you screw up, why did you get caught.* Lenny got pinched in Belmont and always talked about how smart the cops were there (they had to be smart to get him, his smile implied). Prison was crime college, with seminars and tutorials held by older cons who analyzed past mistakes and planned intricate schemes for the future, if they had one. Suddenly I didn't have to keep *this* interest secret any longer.

Lenny christened me "Rebel" long before I actually earned the name by acting like one. His reference to my Southern roots, the way he called out "Hey, Johnny Reb" when I walked by, took my foreignness and made affection out of it. I worried about being the lone Southerner in a Northern prison, the guy who didn't know Southie from Charlestown and didn't belong with any of the groups hanging together in tight knots of familiarity. But Lenny joked about it and eventually people saw that my Southern vowels didn't mean I was stupider than they were. And I saw that not being from any neighborhood meant I could hang out with all of them.

Besides the home brew, Lenny's other operation was the wood shop. He made me his assistant, and at the time I would have said that what I loved about it was the money we earned. The shop was a legitimate business; people in the area would deliver furniture that needed to be sanded or refinished and inmates would do the job for about a third of the street price. Manny, a guy Lenny had once robbed banks with, was running the shop when Lenny arrived at Norfolk this time, and Lenny quickly joined him. After a while Manny started saying, "Aah, you and the kid go down this time," sending the two of us down to work in the shop while he lay on his bed. Was he getting lazy? Did he just decide to do Lenny a favor? Whatever the reason, he and Lenny eventually went to the Avocation Officer to arrange an official transfer of the business. Lenny wanted my help or my company, and he paid me out of his own earnings.

The wood shop brought money in and also served as a cover for the pill-running and cigarette sharking I had going all the time. When I walked across the quad carrying furniture, the cops didn't know I was also carrying pills.

"Harrison, can you stand a shake?" the guard would ask. They checked you out like this, as if it was all a playful business. Of course they could shake us down if they wanted to – they didn't need to ask if we could stand it. But I'd say sure, confident that he wouldn't really do it. If he hesitated, the other cop's reassurance was enough. "He's always moving that furniture," the cop who knew me would say, and they'd move on.

So the wood shop was a cover, but in another way, all the business with the pills and the cigarettes and the brew was the real cover. It hid the way the work in the shop was beginning to grow on me. I ran the sanding machine over the surfaces or glued two panels together and tried to see the final product in my mind. The rich smell of the wood, the discovery of my own competence – these were pleasures I kept to myself. But they took hold. They were the beginning of something. Maybe Lenny even understood this without saying anything. Who knows how intentional any of Lenny's offerings were? He was my first prison teacher, but, unlike later teachers, he taught through acceptance rather than challenge.

They got rid of the wood shop a few years later. Said they needed more bed space. Lenny's health went downhill after that, and when he got out of prison he died soon after. I think of him now when I'm doing any kind of woodworking. When I'm remembering those early days. When I'm putting any kind of pieces together.

As I walk down the hall to the visiting room I wonder if I'll remember what they look like. But when I see them waiting there, their familiarity is what startles me. Mom, Grady, Joe: my family. They sit on the uncomfortable plastic chairs, and I see in their postures how out of place they feel. They've made this long trip together, and I can't imagine what they talked about in the car or what they told people who asked where they were headed.

Mom's been trying to visit since she first heard my voice calling from the Charles Street Jail in Boston, and I've been putting her off for that long. I see other guys have visits and I see how confused it makes them, trying to live simultaneously in that world and this one. I see the haunted look in their faces sometimes when they come back from the visiting room. What do their mothers remind them of that they don't want to remember? What do their girlfriends press them to say that they don't want to say? I can guess; when I imagine my own mother visiting, I can guess it too well. *Don't bother*, I tell her on the phone. *Save your money.* When she talks to me long-distance I hear the despair catching in her throat and the way she tries to speak around it. Her love is abrasive, scraping against the numbness I've wrapped myself in. I don't stay on the phone long.

I've agreed to this visit now for a reason I didn't tell them. They didn't ask why I finally said OK – they just made arrangements and came. I go to hug them, but awkwardly. The missing piece doesn't slide back into the family so easily. As we sit back down, my mother begins asking what I think of as "prison questions" – all those things people want to know but can never really imagine. How big is the cell, are you in it by yourself, what do you do all day. Each question clamps my mind shut and I can hardly think how to answer. When she asks, "Do they feed you well?", she quickly adds "You look healthy," giving herself the answer she wants. And then she wants to know how I feel. *How do you feel?* she repeats even though I'm silent. I have the impulse to run back to my cell, but I only shrug and look away. *Shit, Mom,* I'm thinking. *I haven't the slightest idea.* Do you think I can remember a day in the past God knows how many years when I've let that question in for more than an instant? You might as well ask me whether I miss driving my car to the beach, because it's the same answer: I don't let myself.

She gives up and glances quickly around the room at the other men and their families. All these angry sons and disappointed mothers and helpless love. I can almost see her calculating the accumulated losses in the room. Then she looks more closely at these men who have done things she doesn't want to imagine.

"Is it a dangerous place here?" she asks tentatively.

"Well, it can be," I begin, and Grady interrupts,

"Honey, it's prison. Anything can happen here."

I relax a little as I remember that Grady knows. Maybe not all the way, but better than any of them. I turn to him and start to ask a few questions about his job, about Kip the dog, about other news from home. Mom listens for a while and then, hearing me ask about a neighbor in Winston-Salem, she suddenly says,

"You don't belong in here."

Oh God. I'm almost sorry now, seeing so clearly what she wants to believe and how wrong she is. No, it's more than "almost" – I *am* sorry, full of a heavy shame that threatens to rise up and suffocate me. I turn it into anger instead.

"I do belong here, Mom," I protest. "I fit in great." I'm keeping my voice controlled but there's an edge to it, daring her to contradict me.

She shakes her head. I don't say anything, but I want to ask: what kind of son did you think you had? What did you think I was doing all those years? These people are like me. I don't have to pretend anything with them.

She tries again: "You had to be on something." She's reaching now, hoping to find something mitigating. Maybe I did it but didn't *really* do it, not with all of me. But no. I may have been on something most of those years but I knew exactly what I was doing that day, and I tell her so. I've lied to her so easily and so often, why can't I soften the truth about this? Part of me must want her to know it the way I do, to live with the hard stone of it crowding the heart.

She looks at me but says nothing. Joe, who has listened quietly the whole time, takes over and asks, "Why do you think you were so angry?"

"I don't know," I say flatly. "I just hate people. I just don't care about people."

After that there's very little any of us can say.

Poor Joe. It was such a reasonable question, and I was so far from being able to answer it. Self-examination wasn't anywhere on my agenda, let alone figuring out how to change. I'd been coasting for three years in Norfolk, putting all my old strategies to work and finding that wherever I was, on the street or behind these walls, those strategies held up about the same. Which is to say, they worked for a while, and then they didn't. You can put all your energy into running and not thinking for only so long. What Joe didn't know was that a restlessness was beginning to kick around inside me. It was an unfocused irritation and all it said was *this isn't enough, this isn't working.* After three years of the same thing in Norfolk I was straining against the bars, straining against the limits of each boring day. All I could think to do about it was find a way to leave.

Here's the real reason I'd agreed to a visit from my family: I was planning an escape, and I thought this might be my last chance to see them.
I told myself it was a sure thing – I'd use everything I knew and do this
right. I didn't think about what would happen afterwards. Didn't imagine the life of a fugitive too closely. It was all about, it was *only* about,
finding a way to get out.

I hooked up with a couple of other guys and we started planning.
But before we could make the move, another guy ratted on us and we
were picked up and put in the hole. When they held the classification
review hearing, I saw how little they had on us – no actual evidence, just
the word of this informant. They announced that I was being reclassi-
fied to Walpole, maximum security. It didn't even matter that it was true,
that I was guilty of what they said. As far as I could tell, the same thing
would have happened if I'd been innocent. They could do whatever they
wanted, to any of us.

It was a short trip in the van to Walpole. The difference between
medium and maximum is in the height of the outside wall and how controlled the movements of the inmates are inside, but the differences
between Norfolk and Walpole were everywhere in the long sterile hall-
ways, the way it felt like you were being led deeper and deeper into a cage,
the smells of stale bodies and urine and "bullfrogs" – Styrofoam cups of
shit that the men had thrown in anger – spattered against the walls.

It was time for something new. I'd been right about that.

In a dark time, the eye begins to see. Walpole was the darkest, the end of
the line. It was as far away as you could go and still technically be living
on this earth. And it was where I began to pay attention, began to wake
up to myself.

They put me in 2 Block, known as Death Valley because it was where
the hardest and meanest guys got sent. "They're hoping we'll all kill each
other," the guy in the next cell explained when I asked about the name. I
was supposed to be on Departmental Segregation Unit – DSU – status,
but instead of sending me there right away they made a mistake and let
me out on the block, with the general population, and according to their
own rules, they weren't allowed to take it back and send me to the seg unit
after that. I knew enough by then to know that this was a screw up. So
instead they made me do the seg time right there. They kept my door

locked and only let me out on the block an hour a day, and when the other guys would come by my cell, I'd joke, "I'm doing seg time, will you step away from my cell." It didn't make much difference to me. I had no idea yet what real seg time was like.

One of the first things I noticed in 2 Block was Sean. He lay on his bed staring at the ceiling, looking like he was lying in his casket just waiting for the dirt to be thrown down. They opened his cell door, they shook down the cells, a fight broke out on the block – none of it made any difference to him. I thought *I* didn't care, but this was something else. Worse than anything I'd seen.

When you did get a look at his eyes they made you think of a man who'd been to war. A man who expected to be hunted down. Occasionally he exploded into feeling, but it was always anger – *fuckin'* cops, this *fuckin'* block – each word like a punch. I thought *I* was angry. But I liked his honesty. He didn't throw any kind of smile or bullshit over his bare misery.

He wouldn't let me give him anything. I kept asking if he wanted my TV, my radio, a book, something from the canteen, but he never took any of it. It got to be a project for me, to keep trying. I couldn't have told you why, but I had the idea that it was important to get through to him. That something would happen for him if I could, or something would happen for me. I kept throwing him a line, even though he gave no sign of wanting to be rescued.

Grab it, Sean, come on, come back. I'm doing for you what I can't even dream of doing for myself.

Morning after morning it's the same. I call a greeting over to him and I always get the same response:

"How're you doing?"

"Do you really give a fuck?"

I shake my head, not knowing whether to laugh or go down to his cell and try to knock some sense into him. *Sean, give me a break, I'm trying here.* But you have to admire that stubbornness.

Then the day comes, and there's no reason today should be any different, but I call down "How're you doing" and he calls back "Doin' all right. Yourself?" and holy shit I could be laughing now, it's like a sunny day after months of rain, but inside me I'm more than laughing. I'm feeling something and I couldn't tell you what it is, but the way it opens inside my chest makes me think it's almost like crying. All I know is I wanted to see something and now, just for a minute, I've seen it.

I wanted to see if rescue was possible. If you really could come back, if it made any difference to relent a little and let someone else in. People tell you to get your own shit together before you try to help someone else, and that sounds like good advice. But the truth is, sometimes you're the *last* person you'd ever want to believe in. Sometimes you've got to try things out on other people first in order to discover what's possible.

Once Sean opened up to me, we kept talking. We talked about politics, what we read in the newspaper that day, how we felt about the lies and hypocrisy we saw all around us. He started to let me give him things – a packet of instant Cup-o'-Soup, a book I was reading. "I'll pay you back," he always said, and I'd tell him, Sean, I have plenty of soup here. I don't need you to pay me back. I have enough to spare.

As if that wasn't the newest idea to me too. As if I'd ever felt I had enough of anything to spare.

When we ended up in the segregation block together and couldn't speak face to face, we wrote letters, throwing them down the tier so they landed in front of the cell. Right away I signed them "your friend," but Sean resisted there too. He wrote his name without any sign off, and I'd mess with him about it, asking when he was ever going to end his letters the way I did.

"We have the *makings* of a friendship," Sean would answer carefully, meaning don't push your luck. We might get there, but by my standards we're not there yet. When I finally got a letter signed "Your friend, Sean," I started making a big deal out of it, yelling "Hey, what's this at the bottom of the letter, are you sure you didn't make a mistake here?"

"You can read," he yelled back. "You see what it says."

He wouldn't admit it was a breakthrough, but I could hear the smile in his voice. And down at my end of the tier, with all those walls and other men in between us, I was smiling too.

Sean's father was missing like mine was, but he thought I was better off. "At least you knew your father," he'd tell me. If you asked Sean who his father was, he'd say "Some cop my mother slept with." He didn't know the man's name, and he could hardly even call his mother by name either. He told me how she left him tied up in the yard for hours when he was little, and he said it with almost no emotion in his voice, like he was just telling me the name of the neighborhood he lived in. Yeah, I knew that neighborhood. Even as I was thinking *shit, that's worse than anything my mother ever did,* I was also thinking that I knew what it felt like to have your mother leave you alone.

Sean was matter-of-fact, too, when he told me how he'd hurt another kid badly enough that they decided he needed to be sent away to a juvenile facility. "Maybe I'm just evil," he said.

"You're *not* evil," I told him. "You were a little kid yourself. *You* were hurting too."

Look at that knowledge I suddenly had – understanding and compassion for at least one hurting boy. It was just so easy to see it in Sean. He might be 22 now, just four years younger than me and big enough to be a prisoner on a block like this, but some days I could look at him and just see that little kid, a boy who'd been locked up so long that most people forgot he was in there.

Someone's stealing. A pack of cigarettes disappears from a cell, then a magazine, more cigarettes. It makes us all watchful, because we know it could be any of us. When we come back from the yard or the showers, we don't know what will be gone.

One day a guy named Rickrack catches the thief in the act, sees him right there in his cell going through his things, and he's furious. What does this guy think he's doing, sneaking into people's cells? It's a coward's kind of robbery, and it means no one on the block feels safe.

Now that he knows who it is, Rickrack wants to get rid of him. "Will you keep the peek?" he asks me, and I say sure. I'll gladly be his lookout while he goes after the room thief and lets him know we can't afford to have this kind of thing here.

I stand guard while Rickrack gets a broom from the end of the tier and starts beating the shit out of the thief with it, smashing until he's screaming for the cops like he's the most innocent victim around. But at least he's smart enough to be a dry snitch – he yells that something happened to him but he won't say who did it. When the cops get there they see he's injured and they take him to the hospital unit.

But it's not over. A few of the Black guys, the thief's friends, say it must be about race. They say Rickrack just wanted to beat up a Black guy. I make a point of talking to them, a couple of the guys I feel I get along with. "This wasn't about his color," I try to tell them. "It's about the fact that he was stealing." But they're already working up their own version of this thing and they don't want to listen to me. When I get word of what they've been saying, I realize they're blaming another guy for being the lookout – they don't even know it was me.

I'm trying to keep something from happening but then I see that it's just coming, there's no stopping it. They're feeling they have no choice, I'm feeling I have no choice, and Rickrack must see it coming too because he's so scared that he draws heat, making it obvious that he's done something. He's pacing back and forth, looking guilty enough that the cops come over to check him out. When they get close they see he has blood on his clothes, and that's it, they take him to the hole, locking him up in segregation so he can't even stay to finish what he started.

For the next couple of days we can feel the heat in the air. It crackles through the tiers and even the cops know something's coming, but they don't do anything to stop it. They want it to happen. They're bored and curious to see what we'll do to each other, like putting a bunch of natural predators together in a cage and watching them tear each other apart. If they can get us to turn on each other, that's all the more power for them.

The third morning, when I see five Black guys from other tiers come upstairs, I know it's time. They move right to the White kid's cell, the kid they think was the lookout. I know *I* was the lookout, so when they jump him, all five of them, it feels as if they're jumping me. Their job done, they start to head back down the stairs but I run to meet them, ready, and I hear one of them yelling "Rebel's coming up with a knife!"

He's right. I yell *get the fuck out of my way*, and suddenly it's up in flames, everyone jumping into it, 40 guys with knives flashing and blood flowing and then a loud buzz cutting through all the yelling as the cops push the panic button that calls reinforcement to come running in and break it up at last.

By the time it's done, a lot of people are hurt. My cheek and my shoulder blade are cut and I'm taken away in cuffs. I know I'm going to do some *real* seg time this time, down in 10 Block where people can be kept for months or even years. The cops will say I started this riot and in a way they'll be right. In my mind, I had to do it. In my mind, it was the thief who really started it. The thief for stealing, Rickrack for wanting to get rid of him, me for agreeing to help, the Blacks for thinking it was a racial thing, me for insisting it wasn't, the five guys who jumped that one kid, me for coming after them, the cops for knowing and not doing anything until it was too late – how can you really explain what starts something in prison. When you're right in the middle of it it feels like it has to happen, like there's nothing to do but let it heat up and then explode until it ends with blood everywhere and men who are going to get buried even more deeply inside these walls.

But deep inside that crucible was a coil of logic, a chain of reasons that made us believe what we were doing made sense. It seemed obvious to me and my friends that a room thief on the block was an impossible situation. Even though we were thieves ourselves, sent to prison for stealing or worse. When you've got 45 guys on a block and cops you can't trust, you've got to protect what you can. Even guys who break the state's laws have laws they believe in following. Sneaking around, stealing when someone was out in the yard and couldn't confront you directly – there was nothing to respect in that. The straight up way to do it would be to go right in and take what you want in a decent fight. Let the other person have a chance to defend what's his, and if you win it then you've won fair. That's why the way to insult a guy in prison was to say he'd probably had to steal old ladies' pocketbooks when he was on the street. Taking from someone who never could have fought back was nothing to be proud of. There was no honor in it.

I was looking for codes to follow, people to match myself against, the way I always had. I was starting to understand what the old cons would say about the crime that sent me to prison. If they knew the details they'd say it was crazy. There's nothing straight up about sticking around when it's obvious you're not going to be able to just get the money and get out. Refusing to give up, refusing to see the odds, needing to stay and hurt them and play out that whole twisted scene — no matter what I might have said when I was bragging about it, I knew there was no one who would have admired me that day.

So I wanted to learn how to be straight up. But I was still so angry at what gets taken without redress, still so ready to jump in and defend whatever felt like a violation. It seemed like there was no one else who cared, no one else who would do it. Time and again I'd see a man get a sentence like 4-7 years for raping a child, and then I'd see bank robbers get sentences big as phone books. It told me that money was worth more than a child's innocence, to most people. Told me again, because the fact is I'd known it already. I'd known how common the thieving of innocence is, how few are the people who will step up to prevent it.

I was in prison for stealing and about to be sent to segregation for trying to stand up to a thief, and all the reasons and causes twisted around themselves in a tangled knot. Two Block wasn't the worst. I was going deeper in.

There is nothing soft here, nothing remotely like velvet or music or the bodies of women. Only the architecture of punishment and erasure. There is: one bed, a steel frame bolted to the floor with a thin mattress, coated with the heavy, acrid stink of boric acid, the sheets unraveling under you as you sleep, a gray blanket and a flat pillow; one toilet; one small aluminum sink; one stool (but don't imagine anything wooden or crafted; it's steel, too, attached to the wall); another ledge of steel which we call a table; the "TV box," which is the metal cube where a TV would sit if TVs were allowed here; a cardboard box with clothes stacked inside and papers arranged on top. Books go wherever they fit: on the stool, in the box with the papers, under the pillow. Three beige walls, the fourth made of bars, with a slot in the middle for mail or a food tray to slip through. A door of solid steel that can close over the bars, with a small glass window in it. And one man.

This is a cell in 10 Block, the segregation unit of the state's maximum security prison. It sits on a tier of 15 identical cells, with three other tiers of 15 stacked on top. Take the measure of this space: three paces up and three back, over and over again. Stand in the center with your arms outstretched, and your hands just graze the walls. Each day you wake to this. You have only this particular cell, this body confined within it.

The only flesh you touch is your own, the only hands on your body are yours. There is nothing sacred, nothing transcendent about desire in a place like this. If you want to keep this body alive, you will do the barest minimum of what it asks. Its urges are dumb, they don't stop, they don't know how foolish and futile it is to want anything here. You do what you have to do. You subscribe to the magazines, or you borrow them from the guy down the tier. Smut magazines, the security chief calls them, vowing not to let that filth into his prison. Smut, all right, as base as the magazines in your father's house that taught you what you wanted. Embarrassing, some of the guys think, but a necessity here. The imagination dries up, and you need these new images to give you something to crave. The woman is a picture; you are never really with her. It isn't touch, what she's giving you, but don't think about it. It doesn't matter. This is what there is, and all there is.

The only flesh you touch is your own. This is the only transcendence you have, the only prayer you can offer. This place wants you to solidify, hard as the steel you live in. In the half light of the morning, you reach for yourself to prove you're still here. It's lonely work. You stare into the eyes of the woman in the picture; you tell yourself she sees you, *someone still sees you.* You make yourself believe this. And then the release rips through you, shatters like glass, a sweet joy so intolerable you can't think about it afterwards, but for one moment you surrender to it: *yes I want I want I want what I cannot have I am not dead.* The wanting surges through you, out to the edges of the body, the limbs, the skin. Without this, you're nothing, they've won. It looks like yielding but it's really defiance. *I'm still a man,* you tell yourself, and there's both fury and relief in the telling.

10 Block is all about paradox. If you try to see it only one way, you've got it wrong. Desire is impossibly painful here. You have to kill the outside world in your mind, extinguish any longing for it. But the longing is all you have. When so much of you belongs to someone else, passion and fury are how you reclaim yourself each day. These may be opposing realities, but both are true all the time.

A segregation unit is an extra punishment, an inner rung of restraint and deprivation within the deprivation that is prison already. It's a continual subtraction: prison itself takes away liberty, power, respect, and a thousand other little freedoms that ordinary daily life is made of. Segregation takes away more: you no longer eat with others, talk face to face, walk to showers or the library unescorted, meet visitors without a grate in between, attend classes or programs, walk out of your cell without a guard to unlock it and without being handcuffed and strip searched first. Living this way is a prolonged sensory deprivation experiment, yet in a strange way, the senses also become more acute.

When I go back to 10 Block in my mind, I see myself lying on my bed staring at the opposite wall. Vision adjusts to what it's given. There are no windows in the cells here, just the small windows across the tier that let in a precise rectangle of daylight. Distance vision atrophies; when guys get out of segregation, they're often squinty-eyed for a long time. As I sit on the bed, the walls begin to close in; a ring of darkness forms around the edges of my vision, terrifying me into believing I'm losing my sight or my mind or both. I grab a book and see that the print is clear. My eyes can focus on it, and I read a paragraph, letting it reassure me.

Then I hear the sound of the guard's key in the gate, his footsteps on the tier. The particular distinct sound tells me which cop it is. Everything pummels my eardrums, echoes inside me as though my entire body is cavernous and vibrating. I hear the repeated clicking as the cop fidgets with the cuffs he carries on his belt. This nervous habit, common with cops, drives me to an agitation so unbearable I finally yell at him to stop. When he takes me out of the cell, the shackles around my ankles *slap, slap* against the ground, another inescapable sound. My hands are cuffed to a chain around my waist, and an extra length of the chain hangs down behind me. The cop grabs it like a leash, and I yell at him to stop this too.

Outside in the yard, the other men and I run around and around in our separate cages like dogs in a kennel. At least we can see each other and talk directly and see the sky and the trees stretching over the wall to show us what season it is. A hose lets us take a drink of water. Even in the coldest days of winter, we use the hose to drench our bodies, shivering in an ecstasy of sensation, for that moment wildly, crazily alive.

Getting back to the cell from the yard isn't simple. It takes four guards: one at the door to the yard, one coming up behind him to open my cage, one at the door of the cell holding it open, one standing behind him. There's always a guard in sight; there's no moment when you can imagine you're walking freely. With your hands cuffed behind your back, a moment's loss of balance means a direct fall on your face. "Oops," the guard says afterwards, in mock apology. This is the schoolyard bully, tripping another kid just to see him fall. We're all the school bullies here, locked into a continual dance in which your partner must be kept off balance. I can't let any humiliation go unchallenged. On another day, I trip the guard back, tell him never to do that to me again. He doesn't.

During my years there, inmates in segregation units would go for classification hearings every 90 days to determine if they could be allowed back out into population. For years I repeated this 90-day cycle, going before a board of three officials to have my status reviewed, and each time they would conclude that I was still a threat to security. They didn't have to explain how they made the decision. After a while, when the cop came to tell me it was time for my hearing, I'd tell him I didn't want to go. Why go just to hear one more time how bad I was? I already knew I was bad. I'd been proving it for years, and I was proving it here. I couldn't let the hope enter my mind, except as an indescribable longing and frustration, that maybe somebody would be able to see underneath all my badness and fury and find something else there.

Stand in the middle of the cell, with the guards on the other side of the locked bars. Piece by piece, you hand your clothing out to them: shirt, pants, underwear. They search each one. You wait, naked, until they issue the commands. Lift your right foot. Your left foot. Your balls, finally, and you comply, but the look in your eyes keeps something for yourself. Instead of trying to pretend this isn't happening, you stare at them and show that you know exactly what's happening. "Hey, are you liking this?" you sneer at them, and you see their eyes twitch, although they manage not to answer. "Turn around," they continue. "Bend over," and then they taunt, "More, more!" Admit it: there's no part of your body they don't own. There is nothing you have the right to hide. *Is there something about me that allows this?* No, don't even think it. Don't let your mind wander there. You're naked and all you can clothe yourself with is rage. "Are you going to tell your wife you handled my underwear today?" you sneer at the young one as he hands it back to you. You see him flinch, just slightly, but enough so you know you got to him – just as you got to him when he and the other one came to your door and you yelled, "How're we doing today, little girls?" At times like this, you can see exactly what they fear about themselves. When you toss these insults out to them, maybe you know something they don't. Or maybe they know it about you. It's a matter of who gets there first.

I used that knowledge to torment this one cop who delivered my breakfast tray every morning. I'm holding my cup out through the slot and he's pouring the coffee, and with my other hand I reach over and stroke his hand. "I don't know how to say this," I tell him, putting all the sincerity I can muster into my voice. "I've never said it to another man before"– it's all I can do not to laugh but I keep up the act because it's funnier this way – "but I fuckin' love you." He jerks his hand away, splattering the coffee everywhere, and gets the hell out of there. Now the laughter erupts from the other guys on the tier, and I can even hear the cops giving this one a hard time because they know I was joking even if he didn't.

When I saw him again years later, he finally knew. "You were just pulling my leg back then, weren't you?" he said. Yeah, you got it. Took you long enough. But he didn't realize I chose him because he was the kind of guy who would flinch and jerk his hand away in terror. A cop who could have laughed, let it roll off his back, was a cop I never would have bothered to torment.

To the cops it was raw noise, but to our ears, each tone was particular, each voice distinct. You could throw your voice onto the tier and know it would reach the guy it was meant for. He would pick it out, a single thread in the knot of six or seven conversations going on at once, and respond to you as if you were the only two people talking. It wasn't necessary to see anyone directly, to read lips or facial expression or posture. The voice carried it all. When I got out of segregation, it took me years to be able to look someone straight in the eye. It was too strong, too undiluted; it left nothing to the imagination. In our own cells, we were bodies, straining at the seams, working our muscles until the cell walls dripped with sweat. But other people were disembodied voices. Talking, you talked to the air. Only when a cop appeared at the bars, or when a friend was led past on the way to the showers, was there the surprise of a physical presence, sudden and actual. And only when you were out in the yard cages, with wire instead of solid walls separating you, could you see another man's sweat, his working body matching your own.

Some of us had seen the movie *Papillon* on TV when we were still out in population, and we loved the scene where the prisoner sticks his head out the cell door and asks, "How'm I looking?" The guy next to him, staring at his friend's miserable scruffy face, answers, "Wonderful, just wonderful."

We'd do it to each other when we walked by on the way to the yard or the showers: "How'm I looking?" It was a way of making a joke out of the fear: that we were losing track of how we looked. That we were forgetting how to look normal. That there was no mirror that would really tell us.

The 15 of us on the lowest tier didn't even have access to the canteen the way the guys above us did. They could give orders to the cops and receive deliveries like a bag of instant coffee or a box of cookies. For this we named them the cookie tier, and we said it with a mixture of envy and derision. Sure, they had it better up there, but we were making do with less. We had our ways of fending for ourselves. If the system of vertically arranged tiers, each with access to slightly more privileges than the one below it, was designed to make us want to be good enough to graduate to a higher level, it failed. And if the system was designed to make us hate and resent our upstairs neighbors for their comparatively luxurious life, it also failed. Instead, the cookie tier shared the wealth.

If you're on the lowest tier and you wake up craving a cup of coffee – which you will, because coffee smells of normal life and reminds you of the first grown-up tastes you choked down at your mother's table – here's what you do. Each day, the cop delivers your box of toiletries and later comes back to retrieve it. One day, hold on to your nail clipper and hope he doesn't notice it's missing. Stand on the "TV box" – that box of steel that doesn't serve any function except this one – and use the nail clipper to grind a hole in the concrete ceiling. It takes weeks, but who's in a hurry? The dust falls from the ceiling and each day you sweep it up before anyone notices it. Finally, when the hole is big enough, the guy in the cell upstairs will take some of his instant coffee, roll it up tight in a piece of paper, and slip this tube through the hole to you. You catch it, and now you've got coffee.

Not quite. You still need hot water. Take an empty milk carton you've saved from yesterday's breakfast. Fill it with cold water from the sink. Wind some toilet paper around your hand several times, tightly, and then tuck the ends in. This is called a donut. If you've just arrived here and haven't yet figured out how to roll one, a guy from your tier will throw one down to you so you can examine the technique. When you're ready, take the donut and set it on the back of the toilet. Hold a pencil up to your light bulb, where the wire is frayed, so that you create a spark. Use this to light the donut, and then hold the carton of water over it. Take care not to burn the wax carton or melt it more than you have to. When the water is hot, put the coffee in.

There it is: morning brew. Sitting on the bed with it, I could smell the smoldering donuts of other guys who were also awake at 3 AM. I liked getting up that early – it was quiet, and the guards came by only once an hour. Of course, one might appear just as the coffee was ready, and I'd have to throw it down the toilet, squandering all that effort. But it was worth it for the times I could hold that wax carton in my hand and drink the foul-tasting beverage I'd made myself.

Hours later, breakfast would be delivered. Before the cops handed me the tray, one would pour coffee into a cup. Did he imagine I was sitting there waiting eagerly for what he had to offer? Did he think his coffee was the only coffee I'd get that morning? I watched him pour it and laughed inwardly at how wrong he was. I didn't need it. I'd taken care of it myself. I savored that feeling, sweeter than anything coming to me, until they slipped the tray through the slot and were gone.

The chickens on my grandfather's farm, so dumb and trusting and unsuspecting, the 12-year-old boy on a spring night, the people that boy soon terrorized with his own hands. This drama of power and yield was a drama I re-enacted at every chance. I didn't have the words for it, but it was there inside me always, solid steel lodged inside my body. Here in 10 Block, the guards looked at us and saw chickens; they could do whatever they wanted to us. I looked at them and saw how much they wanted us to beg for mercy just so they could withhold it.

Before the day had officially begun, I'd be up and ready. I had to wake up before they woke me up; I couldn't be caught asleep. The sun would not yet have risen on the world outside and I'd be doing push-ups, sit-ups, chin-ups on the bars. I'd push myself to the limit and push the limit farther each time: not 50 or 100 sit-ups, but 500, 1,000. By the time the cops on the morning shift came to open my door, I would be standing facing them, letting the steam condensing on the walls and my defiant posture speak for itself. "Yeah, he's ready," one cop would say nervously to the other, looking at me through the bars but not looking me in the eye.

Each day was an effort not to need anything from them. As often as I could, I'd take a "bird bath" in the sink rather than accept their escort to the shower. When I was angry about the small meals we were served, I took the hunger and make it my own. Instead of begging them for more food, I said "I'm all set" when they came with the food tray, and I wouldn't accept the inadequate meal. "Suit yourself," they shrugged at first, but after a week or more of this steady refusal they wondered how far I planned to go, whether it was time to send someone from the mental health office to look at me. Could anyone understand the power, but also the desperation, in my refusal? I'd sit there fantasizing delicious meals just to prove I was master of my worst hunger. Watermelon, fudge, French fries: I let all the imagined tastes and textures fill my mouth. I put myself in a state of greater need to show how far from surrender I was, how little I really craved their mercy. I look back on it now and think, no wonder I lasted 12, sometimes even 15 days without food. I was engaged in a battle not just with a system I believed was capricious and brutal but with my own worst demons, from whom even the most severe isolation couldn't protect me.

Sometimes refusal is all you have. I'd tried to make my case in other ways; I wrote letters to the tier officers, the sergeant, the lieutenant, the captain, and finally the director of food services. *I'm hungry all the time,* I wrote. *We all are. I've lost 25 pounds since I've been here.* No answer, so one day I refused to give back my food tray when they came for it. My food tray, right – the dangerous weapon, the obvious security threat. If they were that worried about it, they could have locked the solid steel door over my bars and let me keep the tray. But no, they were gonna win this one. We've got this piece of plastic between us and everything is riding on it. No *way* are they going to let me make the rules. And no way am I going to let them take this last thing. If I can't even protest that I'm hungry, if they're going to turn even this tray into a war, then as far as I'm concerned, all my dignity is in that tray and I'll hang onto it that fiercely.

So it begins: "Mr. Harrison, we're ordering you to give up your food tray."

"No."

"We're giving you a direct order to give up your food tray."

"No."

They slam my door and return an hour later.

"Harrison, you're being ordered to step up to the bars and be cuffed."

"No."

What am I going to do with this tray if I keep it? Bounce it around in my cell? What will they do with it if they get it back? Can anyone even remember what the point of this is?

"Inmate has been advised to step up and be cuffed, inmate is refusing, 'move team' is assembled."

They gas the tier. Five or six guards run in and begin attacking me, and I fight back with everything I have. I'm kicked down under the sink; one of them jumps on me with combat boots. I already can't breathe from the gas, and now this guy is jumping on my chest. I pass out and when I come to a few minutes later, I'm on the bed and the cop is kicking my ankles, trying to break them. Then he's pounding my head on the bed and I'm out again. Next time I wake up, I'm being hammered through the door – they're pulling me out of the cell and slamming me against the door as they go. I'm lying on the tier and a whole team of them want their chance at me. They throw me in another room and, beaten as I am, I find strength to resist them. Only as they're pounding my hands with the fire extinguisher does the lieutenant finally come by and tell them to stop. But they're too far gone and they can't stop themselves. The lieutenant has to repeat it as a direct order before they finally back off. "Calm down," the lieutenant tells me. "We'll take you to the hospital."

The nurse says I'm OK. In this place, if your heart's beating, you're healthy. Never mind the boots, the pounding, the gas choking my lungs. Never mind that all this was over a tray. They can't be coddling those men in there. And no one sees what goes on behind this wall anyway. No eyes here but theirs, so anything can happen, anything at all.

My hands cuffed to waist chains, I can just barely reach the book-shelf. I edge as close as I can and pull out a book, glancing to see if the cops are paying attention. They aren't. They've brought us here, the two of us whose turn it is, leading us past the yard cages that are quieter at night than deserted schoolyards. Walking with them, my face lets nothing in or out. The feel of the night air in my lungs is my own secret, as is the glimpse of the starlit sky I catch for a minute before we're inside again. As is how eager I am to get where we're going.

In the library, the cops sit reading the newspaper to bide the time until the hour passes. I'm at the shelves, holding a book in my awkward grasp, and for one long moment I disappear into the pages. The book is called *Great Treasury of Western Thought* and I know I want to take it back with me. This is a hunger I'm going to let myself satisfy.

The hour is almost up so I grab a couple of paperbacks along with the bulky *Great Treasury* and cradle the books in my arms as we head back to 10 Block. There's no easy way to carry books when you're in waist chains. They slip easily, and if one falls there's no guarantee the cop will stop to pick it up. If he does, he might see the title, and even though part of me wants to brag to him about what I'm reading, or challenge him to see if he can understand it, I'm not in any hurry to let him know how much I really want this book.

In my cell, I keep the book under my pillow. Like the gun I used to keep there, and even though everything got blown wide open that final morning when I left it in the motel by mistake, an echo of the impulse still remains. Is it the impulse to keep every essential thing close at hand so I can grab it and flee at a moment's notice? Or is it the need to touch the solid talisman that I believe will protect me?

The mix of agitation and comfort this book offers is nothing I can ever remember books giving me. Nothing like the boredom I felt in school most of the time. It was so easy to quit school at 16, quit pretending to be a normal kid and give myself completely to the drugs and alcohol that made each day an easy slide into night. There was so little in school to hold my attention, quitting didn't seem to matter.

But back in third grade, there was Miss King, who let us order Signet Pocket Books for 45 cents each through a catalog she brought to school. I gobbled up those books and basked in Miss King's attention when she asked me how I liked them. Would she remember that? How many 8-

year-olds did she lose to the numbness and antagonism of adolescence? Did she ever think I'd end up so many miles from home in a Northern prison? But I'm reading again now, and I'd sure love to tell her about it. To tell someone.

I don't know if Miss King could understand that reading in 10 Block is as much an act of resistance as the insults I shout or the push-ups I do to keep my body defiant. I might not have seen it that way if Bobby – a man Miss King would be afraid to run into – hadn't blasted the thought into my mind just before I got sent to segregation.

"You ought to sign up for the GED," Bobby had said. At 40, Bobby had been in prison for 18 years and in juvenile reform schools before that. Nicknamed "Big Head," Bobby was clearly one of the guys who ran the place. I hadn't exchanged more than a few words with him, but I always noticed how he carried himself, like he was claiming the ground he walked on. A whitened stripe cut through the center of his black hair.

I'd seen the announcements for GED test dates, but I dismissed the idea of signing up the moment I considered it. When this experienced old con brought it up, I couldn't write it off as easily, but I tried to make excuses.

"Why should I get involved in their programs?" I assumed Bobby would understand contempt for anything that belonged to the prison.

"This isn't about them, it's about you," he said, looking at me steadily, and I felt something inside me slip, falter. "You have to take the GED to get into college programs. And anyway, what's the big deal? Why are you doubting yourself?"

How did he know? How could he tell that underneath my disdain for official programs was the fear that I wouldn't pass the test anyway? To get away from the discomfort of being seen so clearly, I jumped on another excuse.

"Why would I want college classes anyway? I've probably got 20 years left in here, so what difference does it make if I take college classes or not?"

"I got natural life," Bobby answered. "You think I'm going to let that stop me?"

That was Bobby. He took truth and held you right up to it, squirming and trying to look away, and he kept holding you there, steady, until something settled inside you and you realized you could stand to look. And then the looking showed you something you'd never seen before. Excuses didn't work. Everything you tried to hide from yourself you couldn't hide from Bobby.

I listened to him, and the pieces of prison's puzzle began to rearrange themselves. *There's another way to play it*, said a new voice inside my head.

"Otherwise they win," Bobby concluded, clinching the deal. He must have known he had me then. He must have known his argument was airtight.

When I saw the test I couldn't believe how easy it was. I glanced around the room and wondered if this was a joke, if the other guys were thinking the same thing. But they were working, so I got to work too. A couple of weeks later, a notice came saying that the results were in and we could come down to the school to receive our scores.

I stood in front of the GED instructor's desk while he shuffled through the papers. Suddenly his expression changed.

"This can't be right," he said. "I've never seen a score this high." It took me an extra second to realize he wasn't accusing me of anything. When he confirmed that the score was right, he exclaimed,

"Now we can get you into a college program!"

He was actually happy for me, or at least happy at his own discovery. Back on the tier, the others were less enthusiastic. When I bragged about my high score, I heard, "Yeah, I need to get my GED too." Instead of trying to encourage them, I went to find Bobby. I told him the news, and his smile was real.

"See?" he said. "You didn't even know what was there."

All those years, and I hadn't known what was there inside me. In some crucial way, I *woke up* that day Bobby talked me into taking the GED. Just biding my time was no longer enough. Coping, even just surviving, started to mean something more than what it had meant in Norfolk and for years before that. I went ahead and signed up for a couple of college classes, even though I still didn't trust the whole idea of it and wasn't so sure I could really do well there. I'd barely started the classes when my role in the 2 Block riot got me sent to a place where classes weren't even an option. I could have given up then, but lying on my bed in the crushing boredom that was 10 Block, I found myself reaching back to that conversation with Bobby the way you reach for a lucky stone in your pocket. "You think I'm going to let that stop me?" I heard him saying, as though only a fool would think a life sentence was an excuse to give up. And for all I'd done to earn my "Rebel" name, Bobby knew something about resistance that I only gradually began to discover for myself. They win if you let them decide who you are. You win if you realize that's always in your own power. "I'm going to come out better than I went in," I said the day I arrived in prison. I'd said it, but I hadn't known how many ways it was possible to mean it.

I started with legal theory. A self-motivated interest in the law gets many an inmate to pick up a book and start puzzling out the meaning of the convoluted sentences. Self-doubt would threaten me. Why should I believe I'd ever be able to understand it? But I'd remember the high GED score and I'd tell myself there was more to me than I knew. And there was no hurry. I could fill the hollow hours by staring at the ceiling or by working my way slowly through a difficult text and no one would know the difference. No one would see how long it took me to get through a single page, so embarrassment was meaningless.

I didn't expect that legal material would turn me on to language itself. But I saw how a decision could hinge on the meaning of a single word. I saw that you had to pay careful attention to each sentence or you got lost and had to retrace your steps. By the time I branched out from legal material to novels, reference books, philosophy, I saw that people who put sentences together were building something. Just like we'd built cabinets in the woodshop. Thinking out an argument, they were as smart as I'd been when I planned a robbery down to its last detail.

No one was paying attention to how fast I read, but I started to keep track of my progress, pushing myself the way I made myself do 50 more push-ups. I'd pick up a book in the morning and decide to finish a chapter by lunchtime, or get through a certain number of pages.

Each page had words I didn't understand. As I sat on the bed reading, I kept a dictionary and pad of paper close by. When I came to a word I didn't know, I wrote it down. Later, I had a list of words to look up, and as I read each definition I made myself use the word in a sentence. It seemed like something Bobby would do. It seemed like something a man who was determined not to be stopped by any obstacle would do. So there were no classes available here in segregation. Did I have to wait for the prison officials to provide me with learning? No more than I had to wait for them to provide me with coffee.

And like the illegal coffee, reading was both sweet and bitter. There was the same delicious feeling of being able to take control and *fill* the hours instead of just trying to obliterate them. Sometimes it felt like the doors inside my brain were springing open. But then I'd get so overwhelmed with an idea or a question that I wanted to talk about it, and when I called out to someone on the tier I was often disappointed. "You're crazy," the guy would say. "Why should I give a shit about that, when I'm sitting here in this cell?"

Why didn't they see that giving a shit about things like that was a way *out* of the cell? When they looked around and saw only the four walls, only the exact moment they were wrapped in, they were letting prison win.

So when I couldn't turn to the other men on the tier, I turned back to the words themselves, over and over again. How many times did I read through *The Great Treasury of Western Thought* during the next couple of years in 10 Block? It was so thick, so complicated, it had so much to say to me. Even the chapter titles read like a list of the things on my mind: "The Human Condition," "Honor, Reputation, and Fame or Glory," "Life and Death," "Parents and Children," "The Passions," "Joy and Sorrow," "The Sense and Sense Perception," "Madness," "Truth," "Crime and Punishment," "Right and Wrong," "Moral Freedom," "The Arts of Teaching and Learning," "Courage and Cowardice."

Alone with the quotes from famous philosophers, I made my own meaning out of them. I read Thoreau on civil disobedience and told myself I was right to be going on hunger strikes, standing up to the guards' and the state's abuse of power. Augustine said evils imposed by unjust rulers are tests of virtue, and I thought maybe I could see the beatings and small meals and strip searches as tests instead of as punishments.

And then there was Rousseau, speaking right to me. "Oh, man! Live your own life and you will never be wretched." He talked about how man is always at liberty to acquiesce or resist; he said "it is particularly in his consciousness of his liberty that the spirituality of his soul is displayed." It sounded like Bobby talking about the GED. Like another way of saying, you always have choices, even here. You have liberty of mind and spirit, even here. You know it when you read this book, or take birdbaths instead of showers, or look up words in the dictionary. In all of this there is some kind of freedom.

One way or the other, it was all about waking up. In a cell with next to nothing, what I had was myself. My body they couldn't entirely break, my hunger they couldn't own or satisfy, my mind that was holding private conversations with Augustine and Rousseau. I had the self that was resisting, the self that was fighting back, reading these words, learning how to *think*. I was learning what the 12-year-old boy, the man with a knife, the man in a cell had been trying to find out for so long: no, you *can't* claim someone entirely. There is always some part that no one else can get to. Even when you are invaded, or stolen from, or locked up, there is some part that stays, inviolably, yours.

"Look at me," she says. She needs to remind me because I go for days here in segregation without meeting another person's eyes. Even on visits, I can slip into my own mind until Anna draws me back. And she does, again and again.

Anna had something and I wanted it, God how I wanted it. So much that if I really opened myself to it I might never be able to close up again, so I had to be careful. I stared at her on those visits as though staring would quench me, and then I couldn't stand to look anymore because looking reminded me of just how thirsty I was.

Her eyes had caught me the first day I met her. We were at the party for GED graduates, a party I wasn't going to go to until Richie talked me into it. He was a good friend, about my age, crude and mischievous but decent underneath. He asked, "What's it like in North Carolina?" like he really wanted to know. When I got the highest score on the GED, he was one of the few guys who seemed to have enough happiness to spare some for me. The day of the party, he saw me lying on my bed like I had no plans to go anywhere.

"Aren't you coming?" he asked.

"Nah," I said without even looking at him.

"Why not?"

"Why should I?"

I was always challenging other people to give me reasons. Bobby might have convinced me that the GED could be mine and not theirs, but going to a party thrown by the education officers of the Department of Correction was pushing it a little too far. It seemed like a joke to me. Were we little kids in party hats? Were we even ordinary high school graduates in caps and gowns?

"Oh, come on," Richie kept at me. "You can sit with me and my family."

Were people constantly making lucky guesses, or were my real feelings that obvious even when they were a mystery to me? My own family wouldn't be there, and OK, maybe I didn't want to sit around with a bunch of guys whose mothers had shown up.

"How can you not show up when you're the valedictorian?" Richie wanted to know, so incredulous he snapped me out of my self-pity. All right, I told myself. This isn't about failure, for God's sake. I aced the test, and I might as well go there and accept it.

Richie introduced me to his mother. She smiled at me and her blue eyes were electric. I looked at them, looked away, and then wanted to look back and keep looking. I thought things you weren't supposed to think about someone's mother. *You're just desperate*, I told myself. All this time without seeing a woman who isn't a cop or a nurse or part of the system some other way. That's all it is. So I sat with Richie and made small talk with Anna and never expected to see or hear from her again.

Months later, I'm in Norfolk, awaiting official sentencing to 10 Block as punishment for the riot. So much for the possibilities the GED promised. I'm on seg status now and will be for a while. When the cop comes by and says, "Harrison, you've got a visit," I'm sure he's wrong. It can't be my mother, and there's no one else who would come.

"Better call back down," I tell him. "It must be a mistake."

But it isn't. I go to the visiting room, and Anna walks in. She hugs me hello, and I'm totally confused: what is she doing here? I ask her straight out.

"Richie asked me to come down and see how you were."

"I'm all right," I say, still taken aback. She sits down, and I think, what a friend Richie is, to send his mother over to Norfolk just to see how I am. But what kind of woman is this, visiting not only her own son but another woman's too?

We make some small talk now, awkwardly. I don't know how to do this anymore. I have none of my old lines. But I start to remember how I used to just come right out and say it with women, so after a while I look right at her and say,

"Did you feel the same way I did at the party?"

What balls, right? To assume she felt the way I did, to imagine she could see me as anything but a kid like Richie. But once the words are out of my mouth I feel some of the old cockiness return.

She says, "What are you talking about?" and I think maybe I've blown it. But I push on, reckless as ever.

"I'm talking about the magic I felt when I saw your blue eyes."

Her expression softens and all at once I know. I'm not crazy.

She nods slightly, and we sit smiling at each other. Then the hour's up and she asks if she can come back again.

"Do you want to?"

"Yes, I do."

I knew it. I asked just to hear her say it. Walking back to my cell, I feel lighter than I have in a long time. I've got someone who wants to come see me. She likes me too, I say to myself, and it's got all the giddiness of a first crush. But soon enough I'm lying on my bed thinking about it and another voice inside me says *are you out of your mind? This is Richie's mother.* And I lie there wondering if I've done an incredibly stupid thing.

She started visiting on Saturdays. She kept coming until I got moved to 10 Block and then she still kept coming, even though visits there meant looking at each other through an iron grate. Richie knew she came to see me, but for a long time he didn't know that there was anything more to it than his mother's kindness. She had two men on the inside now. Two men to write to and visit and worry about. And love.

What kind of woman would love someone like me? This fragile bird of a woman was steadier than I'd known people could be. What was the matter with her? I asked myself more than once. What kind of woman would want a man who couldn't touch her, couldn't give her anything but an hour every fifteen days, trapped in a room with a guard watching? She was crazy for loving me, or she was the most amazing woman who ever lived. One or the other, but either way I couldn't figure it out. Some days I just let myself accept it as the gift it was. Some days I put up my hands to block her love before it even reached me.

The first day she came to visit in 10 Block, I was angry at her loyalty. Stubborn, I thought, and stupid. Who would choose this?

"What the fuck are you doing here?" I demanded the minute she walked in. Do you get off on punishment? I thought but didn't say. Do you like this more, the worse it gets?

"You don't need this shit," I went on. "You can walk out of here and find someone else."

"I want to be here."

Anna wasn't going to be the one to leave. She knew so much more about staying than I did. Maybe I didn't want to find out how little *I* knew, or how little I would be able to give back. Maybe I could tell even then that this was going to end badly. Maybe I didn't want to stick it out just to learn how damaged I was after all.

I gave her every chance to get out, but nothing deterred her, so finally I said OK. Don't say I didn't warn you, and don't blame me if you end up sorry later, because I'm telling you right now: I promise nothing.

So many warnings and disclaimers, and underneath all of them lay something it would be years before I could really see: I was also saying *prove me wrong.* Prove I *am* someone worth hanging on for.

We had been careful in Norfolk, still getting to know each other, still unsure what all this was going to mean. Now we sat with an iron grate between us and I couldn't believe I hadn't touched her when I had the chance. Now I thought I would do anything to melt that solid barrier so I could hold her in my arms.

But there were paradoxes even in this. With Lisa, I had wanted to crawl inside her, to possess her so totally that I would be without want, without emptiness. And look what happened then: the wanting reared up and hit me in the face, mocked me for even thinking I could be still and satisfied. Now, with Anna, wanting was all I had, so I crawled inside *it* and tried to stay there. The grate forced me to live inside desire because there was nowhere else to go.

One day she told me she was breaking up with Hal, the married man she'd been seeing in secret. Being involved with him made Anna feel guilty but it always made me feel *less* guilty, because if she had someone else it meant I didn't have to think too hard about what I couldn't give her. Hal might have been married, but there was no iron grate between them. When she said she'd decided to leave him, I protested.

"You don't have to."

"But I want to."

What she always said! Anna liked to feel herself loyal, able to come through for me all the way. But it seemed crazy for her to swear fidelity to me, and I told her so. "It doesn't make sense." For you, I meant, but I also wondered if it made sense for me. Could I really bear the weight of being the only man she had?

"I wasn't getting what I really wanted from him," she said, closing the book on Hal for good.

She wasn't? Well, it was true. Hal gave her sex but not much else. I couldn't sleep with her or even hold her but I could listen to her for an hour and make her feel she was the only woman in the world. I could write to her every day, spilling my thoughts, writing so graphically about what I *wanted* to do to her that in some way maybe that was good enough. Loving a man in prison is a strange thing. He has less to give in some ways, more in others. For some women, especially women who've been hurt before, the equation balances about right. A man in prison has all those hours with nothing else to do but think about you, and then in the visiting room, suspended in that space that is not exactly prison and not exactly the street, it's as if nothing else exists but the two of you.

We spent more time talking about her than about me. There were a lot of things I still wasn't ready to tell anyone. But maybe she didn't want to know too much, either. Didn't want to know what makes a man end up in prison.

I tried to fill myself up with her so I could take her back to the cell with me later on. At night her letters would drop through the mail slot and I'd let them lie there so I could wake to them in the morning and conjure her with me. But it didn't always work. The isolation of 10 Block was cold and internal and sometimes it seemed impossible to believe she was real. My imagination couldn't do it, couldn't make her solid in my mind, and I would have to reach for the magazines instead.

Eventually we had to tell Richie. Anna said she couldn't keep it from him any longer. By then Richie and I were both in 10 Block and I wrote him a note so I could say all I had to without anyone else listening in. I told him things between me and his mother were more serious than we had made it sound. I said I didn't mean for things to happen this way but they did, and maybe I screwed up but I hoped he would understand.

"How could you?" he wrote back. "If you saw it going that way, you should have stopped it. Out of respect for me, you should have ended it."

Maybe he was right. It was hard for Richie, no question about it. "Rebel's involved with your mother?" the other guys asked, and he didn't like the way it made him feel. Who wants to think of their mother that way under any circumstances? And I was his friend, only a couple of years older than he was. He *knew* how I thought about women. He knew what it was like here.

I felt like I'd violated a code of prison friendship. But in a way, prison also protected us. It was harder for us to fight about it than it would've been on the street, and Richie didn't have to see his mother with me. All he had to do was hear about it and see how happy it was making her. "I deserve this," Anna told him, and it got to be hard for him to argue with that.

It took a while, but eventually Richie saw that he wasn't really losing anything. I knew it was OK when the two of us could finally joke about it. "Your mother snagged a 25-year-old," I teased him, and he actually laughed. It was weird how things worked out, but this wasn't the worst that could happen. In the end Richie probably realized we all needed whatever love we could find.

The years passed, and Anna kept coming, no matter what prison I got transferred to. I got sent to federal prison in Pennsylvania for a year and she still made it there a few times, and then I came back to Massachusetts and Richie got out of prison but Anna still came to see me. More and more, she arrived out of breath. She had to sit for a while before she could talk. It was the emphysema she'd had from the time I met her, getting worse and worse, ravaging her lungs until I began to feel that she wasn't going to make it. She never said anything; I just felt it and I can't even explain how I knew.

Did I stand by her, be her lifeline the way so many times she had been mine? I wish, God how I wish the answer was yes. But I didn't. Her illness terrified me and I ran the only place I could go: deeper into myself. What I told myself was that I was worn out, couldn't take any more, and besides, I couldn't really help her anyway. What I told her was that I needed to cool things off — I just didn't feel it anymore.

So many ways we try to fool ourselves when we just don't have what it takes to hang on.

I can gnaw on it forever, this hard bone of regret. It sticks in my throat, it blocks the tears I ought to cry for her, and still I can't let go of it. I didn't touch her when I could have, I didn't know how to say I love you and mean it the way she did, and when I knew she was dying, I pulled away instead of moving closer.

I can find any number of things to blame it on. I can say she knew from the start that any man in prison is only half a man when it comes right down to it. I can say that I'd lost too many people already and couldn't afford another. I can say that I couldn't have been at her bedside anyway. Prison rules have no mercy, and even if I'd begged and argued that death gives no second chances, I'd still have been talking to her on the phone instead of holding her hand. So what does it matter?

She knew the difference, though. She knew it wasn't only prison that kept me from her. Even if there had been no grate between us, I'd have thrown up a barrier of my own making. I looked at her and knew she was dying even though she never said it out loud. I saw the storm coming and I panicked. The cop said she was here and I refused the visit. "Tell her to go home," I said, and she went but never gave up. "Why can't I see you?" she asked in a letter. She wasn't embarrassed to keep asking. Would I ever, ever lay my own need so bare?

Finally from a safe distance I was able to talk to her sometimes, even to see her, but it was never the same. I'd made that clear. And she *was* dying. Every time I called Richie on the phone I knew it. "My mom's blind now," he said, and for a minute I let myself picture those eyes not seeing. Blind, skeletal, unable to write letters or visit anymore, she still kept saying she loved me. She was always that stubborn; she was always that sure.

One day on the phone I knew it was the last time, but how can we ever handle knowing that? How can we ever say goodbye? Later Richie told me, "Once she got that call from you, she was at peace."

Prove me wrong, Anna. Is it possible, just barely possible, that she loved me because there was something in me worth loving? What did she see? I'd come to the visits cuffed and shackled, caged like a strange zoo animal and just as wild, rocking back and forth and spewing hatred. She looked at me and saw past all of it. With her steady gaze, she found a calm place inside me and she kept holding on until I felt it too. Maybe that's what peace is, that knowing and the faith that another person can find the same knowledge.

So often I said she was crazy. So often I believed I was crazy myself. Maybe we *were* crazy, but only as crazy as any fools who've been beaten down but dare to get up for another round. When eventually I did get up again, I was different because I had what she left me. I had emptiness and fullness both; I have them both still. The regret and sorrow eat away at me, but her gifts rush in to fill that space. And then recede again with my grief and guilt, and back and forth it goes. Like waves, Anna, breaking over me whenever I think of you, crashing and foaming until I think I'll be knocked down. But I'm not. In the end I stay standing, Anna, I stay holding on.

For a while in 10 Block, the guy in the next cell was named Danny. He was younger than I'd been when I came to prison, and what he knew about himself was his toughness. No one wanted to mess with him, including me. But I wasn't so afraid of him that I shut him out entirely. Sometimes we stood at the bars and passed the time by talking back and forth.

"Reb," he said to me one day. "You know a lot about a lot of things. Where'd you learn so much?"

"Mostly from reading."

By then it was true, and anyway I could tell that was the kind of knowledge he meant. He wasn't talking about what I'd learned on the street, things he knew as well as I did.

"You know, I don't read that well," he said quietly.

"That's OK, I didn't either at first. You probably just need practice."

I could feel him listening, and I had an idea.

"If you want, we could read through the newspaper together and you could practice that way."

It was just gut feeling that made me suggest that to him. He'd shown me weakness and I could have ripped it apart and thrown it back at him. I could have turned away from him because I still hated the soft under-belly of surrender no matter where I saw it. But I was reassuring him before I had time to think about it. Whatever made him blow his cover with me likewise made me want to look and see what was revealed.

I had something Danny wanted, and I actually looked forward to the challenge of trying to pass it along. I already subscribed to *USA Today* and saw plenty of other newspapers and magazines. We all traded them, tied with a line of dental floss or shoelace or a thread from the bed sheet and hurled through the bars. With good aim, you could make the "kite" land right in front of the friend it was meant for, but the line gave you the control you needed if the object at the end accidentally got wedged against the opposite wall. I could easily have passed Danny my copy of the paper, but I thought it would be good if we each had a copy so we could both read the same thing at the same time. I thought he should start with short articles rather than with the books I was reading.

Danny asked his father to get him a subscription, and when it started coming, I had him read an article aloud. His reading wasn't terrible. He could sound out most words, but sometimes he'd stumble and it was obvious he was just mouthing the word without understanding it. I stopped him.

"Do you know what that word means?"

"Kind of," he said, hedging. I knew how much time I'd spent looking up words in the dictionary. I knew you could go from ignorance to knowledge if you stopped bluffing and admitted it. So I said, "Hey, it's more important for you to tell me what you don't know than to try to cover it up."

He started to ask me about the words. I'd read an article aloud so he could hear what it sounded like when it was read fluently. When Danny read, he didn't notice punctuation or didn't know what it was telling him to do, so as I read I explained that I was pausing here at the comma, pausing longer now at the period.

After a few weeks of this, Danny greeted me in the morning by asking me what I thought of an article about the Middle East in yesterday's paper. I hadn't read it, and he laughed, tickled that he was now reading more than his teacher. Of course I went back and read it so we could talk about it together.

There was more to Danny than he knew. I saw through his toughness just as Bobby had seen through mine – I saw that he terrorized everyone else to hide his own fears. When he got out of prison a few years later, he wrote me a letter saying, "I can't thank you enough. You taught me things about myself I didn't even know." Almost word for word what I'd say to Bobby now. Bobby had thrown a chemistry book down the tier to me and it landed with a thud of challenge and belief. Danny and I stood at the bars holding our newspapers and reading aloud. Segregation was designed to keep us from each other. In 10 Block, almost anything you have in a cell or pass to someone else is considered contraband. We did trade drugs, makeshift knives, illegal coffee, smut magazines. We also traded a contraband the cops couldn't imagine: the idea that what we were now wasn't all we'd ever have to be.

Danny's grateful letter would have been the perfect ending: confirmation that what I tried had worked. But the letter outlived him. By the time I sat reading it, he was already dead, killed in a stupid drug-related incident that stamped "Null and void" over the hope the letter expressed.

It was his girlfriend who mailed me the letter and broke the news of Danny's death. Her name meant nothing to me, but a cop told me she'd been calling and calling, trying to speak with me, so I called her back and she said she was Danny's girlfriend.

"I feel like I know you," she said. "Danny's talked about you so much."

"What's up?" I asked her, already worried.

"Danny was killed today," she said bluntly, and I could hear in her voice how much she wanted us to grieve together. I couldn't. I was so tired of bad news that all I felt was the familiar numbness. I stared at the beige wall and tried not to think.

"I have this letter he was about to mail you," she was saying. "It's all stamped and everything. I don't know what to do with it."

"Send it," I told her. "Go ahead." I said it more to get off the phone than anything else.

If only I'd had a chance to read that letter as he meant me to, thinking he was doing so well and I'd had a hand in it. Did his death make a mockery of everything he learned? Or should I be glad that at least he discovered those things about himself before he died?

Without answers to these questions, what I'm left with is what I saw in him. "We teach what we want to learn," the saying goes. I was sick of bad news and sick of being reminded that it was stupid to expect anything more. For a while afterwards, I kept myself aloof from people, especially from guys with short prison sentences who were going to get out soon and put me at risk for getting phone calls like the one from Danny's girlfriend. But I couldn't turn all the way back. There *was* something more. Bobby saw it in me; I saw it in Danny. And once I'd seen it, I couldn't forget it.

Danny's mother was a drug addict. She left him in his crib, a three-year-old, too big for a crib but way too small to be left alone. He couldn't get out, and after days with nothing to eat and no one to change the clothes he had long since soaked through, he was finally rescued. Someone must have found out that his mother was gone and the boy was there all alone, because his father heard about it and came to get him. His father kept him and raised him, but those days in the crib must have burned a hole of neglect in Danny that nothing could ever quite fill. Whatever amends his father tried to make never really did it for Danny, because twenty years later he was looking out another set of bars, just as trapped.

He had told me this story during one of our conversations. Sitting in our adjoining cells, we couldn't see each other but he knew I was listening. Even with all the noise on the tier, the clang of the gates and one guy's holler ricocheting off the walls, I was listening. It was strange: so much of what Danny felt toward his parents was what I felt toward mine, but in reverse. He was desperately angry at his mother for leaving him and stuck in a mix of resentment, gratitude, and shame when he thought of his father, who had saved him from that abandonment but hadn't managed to save him from himself. I thought of Danny's huge, brutish body, how disinclined I'd been to get anywhere near him. There was so much more to everyone than met the eye.

It overwhelmed me, sometimes, what unaddressed misery lay underneath the armor we all wore. We were crustacean: the hard skeleton on the outside covered such soft and unseen flesh. When you pried open that outer wall, what you saw was almost too terrible to look at, but like a traffic accident the sight kept drawing you back: How did this happen? Can anything be done?

I started to think of myself as the man with the big bag of secrets. I became someone who could hear anything and who tucked it all away and never betrayed a confidence. Of course, kicking around in that sack were secrets of my own. For a long time, I listened to everyone else but volunteered very little information myself. I was something of a mystery man and I liked it that way. It was several years before I decided it was time to reach into the bag and pull one of those secrets out.

When I decided to do it, it was conscious and premeditated. I was watching television one day, just idly flipping through the channels, when I stopped at The Oprah Winfrey Show. She was talking about sexually abused children that day. The guests told their stories and one man gave figures, explaining how common such experiences are. The simple arithmetic of it hit me full force. Think what this means, how many people this has happened to, and therefore – therefore! – not just to me.

Not just to me. I was riveted to the television set; I doubt I'd have heard if a fight had broken out next to me. Oprah looked right through the set and into my cell, and she spoke directly to me. The raping of children is something that happens. A terrible thing, yes, but not something so extraordinary that it has no name. There is nothing so specially bad about you. What happened to you is solid, knowable; it is nothing more than a fact in this world.

If people were talking about this, then there must be words for it. There were no words in the boy's throat that day when the man wrapped his hands around it and threatened to break his neck if he ever told. There was only the thickly sweet smell of the honeysuckle, now sullied by the stench of fear. And there were no words later, when I got to the bar and looked into my uncle's huge unforgiving face and my mother's hard, accusing eyes. Are there kids who run home from danger into the firm weight of their parents' bodies, knowing they'll find comfort there? Maybe there are, but I had never been one of them.

There were no words then or later, only pictures burned into my mind: the helpless chickens who surrendered their fate again and again, their trust shot through with betrayal. I kept holding those pictures up to people whenever I had the chance, saying, "See? This is what I mean." But the people only stared back blankly.

Now I learned that there were words and maybe, just maybe, if I used them what I said would make sense. I knew that if I was going to tell anybody, it would be Sean. Sean and I had been through so much together since that first day we met in 2 Block. Even more than with Danny, I'd seen past the outer crust into the molten core, and I realized what a responsibility that kind of vision was. Sean was as hurt inside as anyone I'd known. But we also trusted each other more than I'd ever thought possible.

In the old days, when I saw trust or anything that even looked like trust, I only wanted to annihilate it. When I saw that open, exposed place in people – the look in their eyes that said *help me* or *I need something* or *please* – it was like a mirror in a horror movie; I saw my own face staring back at me, grotesquely magnified and unbearable. I had to get rid of it, and I had to teach people what I knew: this is what it is to believe in safety and find out you're wrong. This is what you do: you make yourself into something that has no openings. Make yourself somebody with nothing left to steal.

So familiar to me, that drama. But now when I listened to Sean, I didn't want to annihilate anything, not even when he told me the worst things about himself. *This is a vulnerable human being*, I said to myself. I thought of the kind of man who would take Sean's trust and rip it apart, shred it until all he had left were ribbons of fear. I thought of the man who would do that, and he looked just like the man who had once raped me. And then I realized something else. *I don't want to be that kind of man anymore.*

Sean had given me so much already. He'd given me that molten core, hot and terrifying, but this time it hardened into something unexpectedly delicate and luminous, something I had to cradle in my hands. And I would. Careful and steady, I would hold this precious thing.

And I began to think about telling him my own secret. Since that day with Oprah, I'd felt myself building up to it, and now these conversations with Sean made me surer and surer that telling was the right thing to do. I had looked at Sean's private pain straight on and discovered I could take it. It was time to believe I could bear my own.

That was the thing about friendship: you did something for someone else and the gift was yours too. Speaking these words aloud was going to be like nothing I'd experienced; that much I knew. It would be like stepping off a cliff – there would be no turning back. But it was time.

There we were in adjoining cells, just as Danny and I had been. Now I was the one appreciating the barrier; I couldn't see how Sean was taking it, but I felt safe. I spoke quietly. I knew I had Sean's full attention, and I knew no one else would hear. I said the words. *When I was 12 I was working at the gas station and this man said he'd take me home but instead of taking me home he took me and raped me.*

There, I'd done it. Sean didn't say much in response, but he didn't need to. He opened his hands and held it.

We woke up the next morning. "How're you doing?" I called over, same as always.

"Not bad. Yourself?"

Sean was still there; I was no different in his eyes. Nothing had changed. Nothing except the lightness, the release that felt almost like flying. I'd jumped off the cliff and a parachute had opened. So many things that I'd thought were true were turning out not to be true at all. Funny how wonderful it can feel to be wrong.

We hear the dogs first, an explosion of barking in the night.

"Rebel, stop that!" somebody calls down, thinking it's me fooling around.

"It's not me," I laugh, and the tier falls silent as everybody strains to hear what the hell it is, then.

"They've got the water turned off," someone else says after a moment. They only do that when they know you're going to be really pissed and they don't want you flooding out your cell. Got to be some kind of major shakedown.

Cops thudding onto the tier, a sound you don't forget easily. More than fifty of them, lining the tier now, filling up all the space. They're everywhere you look, but in their riot gear it's hard to tell one from the other. Blue jumpsuits, padded vests, helmets with plastic shields. They're completely protected. What do I have to protect myself?

You always think they're coming for you, and sometimes you're right. But here's what I have: the fact that I don't care. Nothing's going to bother me. When it was heating up, I was tensed and alert, but now that it's hot and I'm right in the center of it, I'm calm. If you look at powerlessness the right way, you can let it free you: *what the fuck. A cell's a cell. Wherever I'm going, that's where I'll go.*

I've got some grass in my cell and I might as well smoke it, since I'm pinched anyway and they'll get it if I don't use it up now. I light up, stretch out on my bed in my underwear.

One of them sees me. "Hey lieutenant," he hollers. "He's smoking grass in here."

"Who gives a shit?" the lieutenant yells back. The joke's on the other guy, thinking he was right on the ball catching me breaking a rule. Turns out it doesn't even matter; they've got bigger things on their minds tonight.

I'm lying there not looking at anything, but from down at the end of the tier someone calls, "Hey, they're moving people!" OK, so they're working their way down. It'll be a little while before they get to me. I start pulling clothes on, as many as I can grab. I want the layers between me and them, and wherever I'm going, I want as many changes of clothes as I can get. They always say "your property will follow you," but I never count on that.

I yell over to the guy next to me. "If they move me," I say, "will you call that person I was telling you about yesterday?" I mean Anna, and this is how we talk to each other during times like this: in code. Whatever happens, I want someone on the outside to know where I am.

"Step up and be cuffed." Suddenly they're right at my door.

"Where am I going?" I demand, just to see what they'll say.

"You'll know when you get there."

Thanks for clarifying that. I'm cuffed, and the door's open now.

"Face left," the cop says, but he deliberately points to the right. One instant of confusion, I'm like those cartoon characters who don't know which way to look, and they use that moment to snap the leg irons on. Four guys lifting me, hands everywhere, and I'm wrapped in the weirdest embrace I know.

"Where's this one going?"

"Out the door" is the reply from the guy with the sheet of instructions. Out the door and into the car.

All I'm thinking is that we're moving. Let me ride down this road and imagine it's mine, let me turn my face to the black wash of sky, the stars that could be stars from home. I don't care how I'm getting this; I just want to drink it in.

Al interrupts my reverie. We're chained together in the back seat, but he's been in and out of 10 Block so often he doesn't see this ride with the reverence I'm giving it, returned to the world of motion and distance and sky. He's just trying to figure out what they won't tell us.

"We must be going to New York," he says, and then adds knowingly, "Or maybe Connecticut." A while later, seeing the mountains rise from the dark road, he says, startled, "Oh, wait. We're going to Gardner."

Gardner? But that's a good deal, much better than where we're coming from.

Al wants to find out if the cops are stupid. He whispers to me, "If we can make a move, are you with me?" What am I going to say? We're Siamese twins here. If I'm not with him, I don't have a lot of choices.

"I have to take a piss," Al announces to the cop who's driving.

"Me too," I say.

They don't look at us but exchange some kind of glance with each other. The driver nods and says, "We're not supposed to stop, but we will. But no games. If you try anything, Al, we'll shoot."

OK, so these two aren't all that stupid. We get out and it's clear they mean it; one stands with a gun pointing straight at us. But the other disappears and then returns with cups of coffee. He hands them to us and we drink, bending over to reach because our hands are cuffed to the chains at our waists. The night is cool; we don't look at each other or speak. The coffee is bitter but tastes strangely of mercy. The highway stretches out behind us.

Back in the car, even Al has stopped thinking about these cops; now we're wondering what's ahead. We drive up through the woods, and the thought flashes through my mind, *they're going to take us out and shoot us.* Suddenly it doesn't seem impossible, here in the dead of night with the caffeine and adrenaline running through me. The car backs up to the door of the seg unit at Gardner and every light is shining, like we're on the set of a movie. Inside, the corridor is lined with cops and they all wear such nervous expressions I almost want to look behind me to see what they're afraid of, but it's me, all this is for me. It looks like the entire night shift is here.

Into the changing room, and this is familiar now: strip, bend over, let me see all your hiding places. But they leave and I'm alone, wondering how long before they take me to the cell. Then I notice the toilet and sink. *Holy shit, this* is *a cell.* It's so much bigger than the 10 Block cells, I didn't realize it at first. I start pacing around, taking the full measure of it, and the cops are looking into the window trying to figure out what I'm doing. I must look like a crazed animal circling the cage. They think it's the confinement doing this to me, but it's the amazing space.

I hardly sleep at all. The bed is so much softer than at Walpole. Out the window, the sunrise spreads over the sky and it feels like a country morning. I see a cat, a groundhog, creatures you don't see out a Walpole window. I watch, entranced.

Suddenly, breakfast. A young cop opens the door carrying a plate of pancakes, so big I think I'm dreaming. This must be one of those hallucinations you get in segregation. For a week in Walpole I've been refusing to eat, but now the hunger comes rushing in, monstrous, and I want those pancakes to be real.

"Do you want your maple syrup heated up?" the cop asks before handing me the plate. "I could throw it in the microwave."

What?

Do I want my syrup. Heated up. He can throw it in the microwave. This has got to be the funniest thing I've ever heard. I stare at him like he's talking another language.

I must have nodded because he goes to heat it, adding, "This is real

Vermont maple syrup."

OK, they're crazy here. This is clearly their preferred method of torment. Any second now, he's going to do something, spit in the syrup.

I watch him, but the syrup comes back to me clear and pure. I pour
it, eat the pancakes. He's watching me just as carefully, trying to see what
I'll do next. He's muscular enough to fill out his uniform but he's not
threatening me. If I let him see how shocking all this is, maybe he'll stop,
so I don't dare thank him. I just eat while I can.

"OK," he says after a while, as if we've been having a conversation.
"You'll be on DSU status, so you have to have someone with you when
you go shower, but just ask when you need someone. Be patient; we'll
get someone as soon as possible."

I don't know how to interpret the kindness I hear in his voice. It softens the edges of what he's saying, blurs them so I can hardly make sense
of any of it. It's as if someone's been twisting my arm back relentlessly
and suddenly lets go. Relief, like mercy, catches me completely unpre-
pared.

He comes back later that day, and this time he says, "Harrison, you're
going out front."

"What for?"

"The warden wants to see you."

Here it comes. I knew it could never be this easy. I don't like this,
but at least I'm back on familiar ground. Two cops flank me as we go
through three gates and up a flight of stairs. Outside the warden's office
is a cop I remember from years ago in Norfolk. I once gave him hell for
waking me up and he's probably never forgotten it. Worse, he's a captain
now. I look at him warily, but all he says is, "Right in there."

The warden stands behind the desk, waiting. I take in his thick body,
his white hair, the steadiness of his gaze.

"Take the cuffs off him," he instructs the two cops who brought me
in. To me he nods, "Have a seat. I'm sorry about the cuffs."

He's apologizing? I shift in the chair; I don't know what to do with
my hands. He introduces himself, looks down at his desk and then up
again, his eyes clear and meeting me straight on.

"I'm looking at your record," he says, and his voice is matter-of-fact,
not accusing. "It seems like you can be a pretty tough character." He
pauses, but not long enough to let me agree or disagree. "All I'm concerned about is how you're going to act in here." Another pause to let
me take this in, and then he says, "I have one question for you."

"What?"

"Are you going to hurt any of my officers? Do any of my officers have anything to fear from you?"

"No," I tell him, and I do meet his eyes. "My beef is with Walpole. I have no reason to hurt your officers. I'm straight up. If they don't fuck with me, I won't fuck with them."

"Man to man, now, you won't give them any problems? Can I have your word on that?"

It's so strange. He's talking like one of us. And he keeps asking me, not telling me. He keeps demanding that I meet him where he is.

"I'm not here to cause problems," I say again. "I'm angry at what I've been through; I'm not angry at anyone here." I've finally learned at least this much about how to be straight up. With cops, at least, I can see clearly enough to understand who I'm really angry at instead of getting back at other people who haven't done anything wrong.

Across the wide desk he leans toward me, and I see his hand coming but at first I just stare at it, as if I've forgotten what a handshake is.

"Man to man, that's an agreement, right?"

I nod and shake the hand.

"If you have a problem, will you call me or the head of security first, before you do anything?" I nod again, and he calls in the head of security and introduces us and explains the deal we've made. Then he turns back to me and explains what segregation means at Gardner.

"You're on seg status, so you have to live in the seg unit, but you can have normal visits, showers every day, regular food, all the normal stuff." He doesn't say it outright, but what I begin to understand is that this guy doesn't actually believe in segregation as punishment. He's got to keep me in the unit because my seg status is beyond his control, but he's decided what seg means in his prison and it sure isn't what it meant at Walpole.

I'm so blown away by all this that I haven't paid attention to the noises coming from the outer office. Now I realize they're having some kind of party, some secretary's birthday, and people are laughing and singing to her and scraping their forks across the plates. "Do you drink coffee?" the warden asks, and I say sure, wondering what off the wall thing he's up to now.

"How do you take it?" This guy is relentless! He just keeps tossing my dignity back to me, over and over, and although I'm startled each time, I catch it and hold on. He gets me the coffee and watches me drink it, smiling a little because he knows he's reached me.

They had shipped us out of 10 Block because they knew they'd lost control and all they could think to do was to break it up somehow, separate us out. In a way they were right: we saw the cops as trying to break us, they saw the inmates as refusing to obey orders, and we were all locked into our positions, caught in a battle neither side could see a way out of. But that warden at Gardner saw another way. That's what amazes me still. He figured out that you didn't always have to fight fire with fire. "Man to man," he said, and reached right through the ring of fire to something else he believed was there. It's what any good teacher does: you believe you see something, but you also know that if you act like it's true, the kid may be startled into believing it too. You put out your hand and he just might bring his up to meet yours.

When the warden had them take the cuffs off me, he explained to me that I'd worn them only because I had to come through the front gate to his office. His office was actually outside the wall, that was Gardner's strange architecture, so when I sat there without cuffs on, I was closer to freedom than I'd ever been. I could have tried to run, and maybe he knew that because he just about told me straight out where we were. But as he told me, he was also apologizing for the indignity of the cuffs, and the entire surprise of it was so overwhelming that I was jolted into not violating his trust. *Man to man.* It plays in my mind like a mantra. What strange and miraculous courage he showed.

And because keeping his word was so important to him, he ended up having to transfer me out when I'd only been at Gardner eight days. When they came to my door and told me I was going, the disappointment was so sickening that I refused to leave until they told me where. "Norfolk," they said, and when I arrived there it didn't take ten minutes for the sign to go up on my door: "Walpole DSU Status, ISO." I was treated as a Walpole prisoner not only on seg status but on isolation. Even though I was out of 10 Block, it was as if they still had me.

When I thought about it later, I realized the warden had done the only thing he could honorably do. Walpole must have called him and said, "Harrison owes us six months of ISO time." He couldn't put me on isolation status and take away the regular visits, the yard time, the showers, everything that he had promised me segregation in his prison would allow. Not without going back on his word. I hated leaving Gardner, but at least I left with my respect for him intact. He never had a chance to explain it to me, but it was as if he knew I would think it over and realize he never broke his agreement. It stayed with me, whole and untarnished, another unexpectedly solid thing those seething days did yield, another talisman worth keeping.

So there I was at Norfolk, on Walpole's Isolation Status, a situation that was actually worse, in some ways, than isolation at Walpole itself. The only book you could have in your cell was the Bible. My property finally caught up with me weeks later, but the books were confiscated as contraband. I read what I could by borrowing from guys who weren't on ISO status, and I carried the books to the shower so they wouldn't get taken in a shakedown while I was out of my cell. I used my nakedness as an excuse. "Hey, don't look at me," I'd say to the cop, to keep him from spotting the illegal book wrapped up in my towel.

One thing *was* better here: the visits. After months of looking at each other with a grate between us, Anna and I had our first contact visit, and the wonder of that first touch was amazing – how hungry we were for it, how we fell into it, stunned that it was actually, finally, possible. The game was to see how much we could get away with before the cops told us to stop. It was so little, but it was so much more than we'd had before. Those were the high times of our relationship, her death still years away.

I was still thinking about the eight days at Gardner. Eight days that had been full of so many surprises. And then it turned out there was a surprise at Norfolk, too. Another Department of Correction employee who didn't act the way I expected.

I'm sitting across from her in a tiny room, but it's not exactly like being with Anna. Whatever Anna says, she says because she loves me. When she reassures me that I'm OK, maybe it's because she doesn't want to be loving someone who isn't. But with this woman now, it's different. Anything she says, she'll say because she's studied these things and she knows. She's a gypsy and I'm here to get my last-chance fortune told.

I run my eyes up and down her body, all the way from her short black hair to the curve of her ankles that I glimpse under her long tailored skirt. I see the slight swell of her breasts under her sweater, imagine how soft the wool would feel under my hands, and it looks like her breasts would just fit –

I stop myself. Yes I'm hungry for this, yes I'm alone with her, but it's really that looking at her this way gives me something to do. Something I understand. Without it, I'm on new ground. It might as well be my first time with a woman because we're about to do something I have no idea how to do.

"What do you want to talk about?" she asks evenly, and I don't know how she manages to ask without challenge and without more gentleness than I can handle. Just calm, just ready.

"I don't know." I'm hunched over now, not looking at her, my legs jiggling wildly because I just don't know, don't know anything, maybe this was a mistake. "What do people usually talk about?"

"Whatever you want. If something's going on, if something's on your mind –"

Am I going crazy? Am I still me? What do you see when you look at me with those knowing eyes? Do you see a human being, a man, am I out of my mind, is it too late for me?

"What's the deal with confidentiality?" I demand, choosing a question I understand how to ask. I sit up in the chair, show her I'm not easily fooled. "Do you rat me out, tell them what I say?" *Because if you do, this deal's off right now.* I don't add that thought, but I'm sure she hears it in my voice.

"No," she says patiently. "As long as it doesn't involve a threat to yourself or to someone else, or a threat of escape, what you say here is confidential."

Do I believe her?

"I hate this," I say suddenly, the words bursting out from between my clenched teeth. "I hate being locked up, I hate these fucking people, all they want to do is keep me in isolation *forever*." My fists tighten against the cuffs. "What I think they should do, they should get their fucking foot off my neck." I spit out the last word and lean back to look at her. She doesn't flinch. She barely even shifts in the chair; it's like she's ready to sit there forever. She doesn't come back at me with her own litany the way another guy on the tier would. Why should she? She's not one of us; she doesn't have our complaints.

For the rest of the hour she lets me rage. "I just want to kill them," I say over and over, and she doesn't take this as a literal threat she's going to have to report. She just takes it, as if her small arms are stronger than they look, as if this cramped room can hold anything, as if nothing is too monstrous to contain.

Two weeks later I'm still raging. I've been telling her everything I can think of that those 10 Block assholes did, and now I'm telling about the time they beat me because of the food tray. "All because of a fucking tray," I say. It's probably the fourth time I've said it. I'm back in the story, reliving it, and every time I come around to the fury of it I explode again. "All because of a tray, and I only kept it because I was hungry."

I'm wrapped in such blazing memory that I hardly see her, but suddenly when I look up I notice she's crying. Oh Jesus she's crying. Inside me something is rocked, cradled, startled, I can't believe it, this stranger is crying for me. I don't feel tears anywhere in me, just a stone weight all through my limbs and in my chest, but when I look at her face I feel so strange, as if her tears could be the river deep within a cave.

"Dwight," she says, and her words are thick. "You're not crazy. There's no doubt in my mind that you have post-traumatic stress disorder, that's why you feel like this, it's not you that's crazy —"

Goddammit, there it was. What I'd come for. The mirror I only dimly understood I wanted, showing me my own pain. My tears on her face.

Like the warden at Gardner, Patricia from psych services at Norfolk showed me that not everyone whose paycheck came from the Department of Correction was automatically the enemy. Sure, I'd known about psych services, just as I'd vaguely known about the GED for months before it occurred to me that it was something I could do. But psych services at Walpole always seemed like a joke to me, or, worse, an ineffective bone the system threw at us after conspiring to drive us crazy.

"Anyone need psych services?" they'd ask, and the scorn inside me would rise: *no, you bastard, I need you to stop reading my mail and leaving the windows open so the freezing air blasts in and locking me 23 hours a day in this foul-smelling cage.*

Locked up again at Norfolk after the brief reprieve at Gardner, I was trying to make sense of it all. I'd first noticed Patricia soon after I arrived. It was a reflex, to look up whenever the gate at the end of the tier swung open, to check who was coming or going. Patricia made me curious: a good-looking woman walking past us, not afraid to be stared at but clearly having somewhere to go. Finally I asked the red-headed guy in the next cell about her.

"That's Patricia, she's with psych services," he said. I remembered that this guy had tried to kill himself not long ago and I figured out that he must have gone to see Patricia at least once himself.

"What do you talk about with her?" I asked, trying to sound only mildly interested.

"Things that bother me," he answered, his voice tight around the words. Yeah, I bet a lot of things bother you, I thought with some disdain, but another insistent chord was thrumming underneath that one: I have things that bother me. Maybe I should try …

I checked it out with Sean, as if it was some new plan we were hatching together. "Why not?" he said. "You're not going to tell her anything, so why not?" He meant I wasn't going to tell her anything that would incriminate anyone. I wasn't going to abandon all judgment and start talking to one of them about whatever crossed my mind. We acted like that was the main consideration, but Sean must have known I was fishing for reassurance. He feigned casualness just as I did. Anything to break up the day, right? But Sean also counted on me to try things for both of us.

I thought they were all in collusion with each other: cops, prison chaplains, social workers, psych services. I thought anyone who wasn't openly criticizing things or obviously working to change them must believe everything was fine as it was. But the warden at Gardner hadn't thought it was fine to keep piling punishment on punishment, and Patricia, crying my tears, was also crying her acknowledgment that she bore some responsibility for the furious man in front of her. That's how it seemed to me, anyway. Instead of trying to make excuses for the department that she worked for, she actually seemed ashamed of what had been done in its name. When she looked at me she had to know that what happened in 10 Block didn't help anyone.

The warden's behavior was probably strategic, intentional, but what

Patricia gave me was her unplanned, empathetic response. It was the fact that she couldn't help crying that reached me, somehow, because it meant that I was human enough to evoke that kind of response in someone else. What came easily to her seemed astonishing to me. What an unlikely miracle that anyone could really know what it was to be me, that anyone's imagination could encompass what I was feeling.

It felt like a miracle, but it was something that had to happen before I could even think about empathizing with the people I'd terrorized. I couldn't hold another person's agony inside my body when I felt like the world had drawn a circle around itself and placed me outside it. I had to be drawn back into that circle first. I had to meet people who could see me when I couldn't see myself, people who insisted you're one of us, whether you can feel it yet or not.

I sat with Patricia and threw the inflamed rage at her and she held it and said this isn't burning, not really. You feel like it's burning but it's really just broken. You feel like you're only fire or stone, but in the middle of that fire is something cool, and if you split open the stone you'll find something else, tears so new you think you can never bear them but you will, you will because I'm showing them to you now, I'm feeling them first and I'm still here.

It took me a long time, but I did get there. I stepped back into that room, first tentatively and then many more times, with people like Patricia who could look and listen and hold. Eventually I split open the rock not just of 10 Block but of all the other things I never told her, all the old sins of omission and commission that, back in those days with her, I could never have imagined talking about. What I did, what I failed to do, what other people did to me or wouldn't do. Inside that rock I found a place I'd never known I could go, and I found out that others could join me there.

I didn't stay at Norfolk more than a few months. When I heard "Pack up, you're leaving," I assumed I was going back to Walpole, but they said no.

"Where am I going, then?"

"I can't tell you."

It turned out to be the South Eastern Correctional Center, part of the prison complex in Bridgewater, where the famous nuthouse was too. It was older and dirtier than any place I'd been to yet, and they had no real toilets, just shit buckets in the cells. Everything moved slowly – it took hours just to get a pencil if you asked for one – and the cops seemed like they expected you to be stupid rather than dangerous.

The day I arrived at SECC, I could see the cows in the fields around the prison as we drove up to the gate. They looked as sick as I felt. Once I settled in I saw that those cows were a joke to everyone, because the milk cartons at chow time came printed with the words, "From our own cows."

"Guess why this milk's sour?" we loved to yell to each other. "It's from *our own cows!*" You take your jokes where you can find them.

Each time I got moved, I let my mother know about it. I hadn't seen her since that one visit in Norfolk years before, but she always sent money and she always wanted to know where I was.

"Why did they move you?" she asked on the phone.

"It wasn't working out for me there," I said evasively. How was I going to explain the riot, or what 10 Block had been like, or any of it?

"When are you going to stop this?"

She meant when was I going to stop acting up. Like all the moving, all the craziness, was my fault only. Once in a while she brought up the idea of visiting again, but I'd tell her to save her money or spend it on something I needed here, like a television. It was as if I could still hear my uncle's voice telling her that those damn kids cost too much. Stay home, Mom, stay home. I thought she'd be glad to hear she didn't have to spend the money on a trip north.

Or maybe she was waiting for me to ask her to visit. Waiting for me to say I miss you, I want to see you, please come. And that I wouldn't do.

They were running out of options. Ever since they'd shipped me out of 10 Block, they'd been trying to find a place for me: Gardner, Norfolk, and now SECC. But I was still on seg status – still, three years after the original riot at Walpole – and segregation at SECC wasn't a long-term option. The security there wasn't designed for it. And I was still classified to maximum security, which should have meant Walpole, the only maximum in the state. But they'd taken me out of Walpole to show they were in control, that I couldn't resist them and get away with it. If they sent me back there, they'd be admitting defeat. There had to be a way to get me off their hands but save face doing it.

Federal prison was the answer. They filed the papers, waited to see who would take me, and Lewisburg, way out in rural Pennsylvania, was the one that said yes. Of course they didn't tell me about it, any more than they'd told me about any other transfer before it was happening. In the 4:00 AM darkness at SECC the lights went on, I heard my door open, and I looked up to see the hall lined with cops. The sight was getting to be familiar.

"Harrison, stand up, put your clothes on," one said.

Because it was so early in the morning, I had a pretty good idea we were going to be traveling a long way. There were four cops in the car and the minute we pulled out I started fishing for the answer.

"I'm going out of state, right?"

They knew I knew, and I took their silence as confirmation. The ride was less miraculous than that first ride from 10 Block to Gardner had been. This time, I was more worried about where I was going. "Can I swim with the big fish?" I wondered to myself as the cops dozed off and the highway sped by. It was another thing to brace myself for. Another proving ground.

Lewisburg was in the middle of a cornfield. It rose out of the empty space in a way that was actually less intimidating than Walpole, but I didn't let that fool me. After a week of observation in the new man's section, I was let out onto the ranges – Lewisburg's name for tiers. A big old cop, waddling down the hallway with keys in his hand and a baseball cap on his head, gave me the welcome as he unlocked the door: "Here's the key, here's the door, and there's the zoo." He motioned for me to step inside, and I looked warily around, knowing that the most violent men were sent here. That's what we'd always heard. The first night, I couldn't sleep until everyone else around me had fallen asleep first.

"You were different when you came back from Lewisburg," Bobby said years later. "The next time we were in a class together I saw you'd changed. You used to be happy to cheat if someone gave you the answers – you were more worried about looking smart than anything else. But then after you came back I remember that someone offered you the answers and you said no, how'm I going to learn it that way? And I knew you were growing up. You stopped bothering with a lot of the old bull-shit and you started getting serious."

He was right. I did come back changed after the year at Lewisburg, though not for the reasons anyone predicted. "I was worried about you going there," Anna had admitted afterwards. She was afraid I'd come back angrier. You didn't get sent to the Feds to come back calmer. It wasn't supposed to be a place to find peace. That I ended up finding it there shows I was always *some* kind of rebel. Or that I got lucky. Or that I was just ready for something different and circumstances came togeth-er in the right way to give it to me.

I got involved in all the usual things at first: selling drugs, running numbers with an older guy we called Slick Jones. He had just returned from Marion, the infamous federal prison in Illinois, and he had been on the FBI's Most Wanted List – just the sort of guy I expected to meet here. I ran into some guys I knew from Massachusetts and realized that seven years had turned me into a Massachusetts man myself. Federal prisons had men from all over the country, and whenever I met someone from North Carolina he expected me to hang out with him. "What're you doin' up in a *Northern* prison?" one of them asked, waiting for me to laugh with him. But I was getting farther from North Carolina all the time.

Like anywhere, Lewisburg had its paradoxes. One of them was Seamus, the generous thief, the philosopher who taught me so much about how to be free but who couldn't survive in the free world himself. When I first saw Seamus in the yard, his big glasses and goofy expression made me laugh, but when we started talking, I liked him. His goofiness just meant he wasn't afraid to ask silly questions or do crazy things right under the warden's nose. One of his capers had us stealing huge blocks of cheese from the prison kitchen. We waited until we saw the warden go into the kitchen and then we walked in right behind him. When his back was turned we picked up the cheese and walked right out again carrying it. The cop outside the kitchen asked what we thought we were doing. "The warden told us to bring these over there," we answered, giving every appearance of obedience.

Seamus loved this kind of thing, and I loved how his enthusiasm outweighed the sheer nuttiness of any idea. "Are you crazy? We can't do that!" I said when he first came up with the cheese plan, but Seamus said "Of course we can," and later, sitting in his cell eating the cheese on Ritz crackers and talking about everything under the sun, I laughed to myself. One thing you had to say about Seamus was that he knew how to enjoy life.

The first time I walked into his cell, I looked at his row of books and noticed some by Edgar Cayce. "Who's he?" I asked, and Seamus said, "He's a healer." For all his goofiness, Seamus could say things like that with a straight face. You could talk about big questions with him and he wouldn't laugh. We sat on his bed and argued about God, about truth, about victory in wartime. All those *Great Treasury* ideas came back to me full force now that I had someone else ready to take them on. Seamus could carry on a conversation for hours, leaping up sometimes to pace the floor or to disappear for a minute and return with cups full of hot water for coffee. (Compared to the "donuts" of 10 Block, coffee in Lewisburg was luxurious: instant coffee purchased from the canteen and hot water from the water cooler at the end of the range.)

Seamus was a thief who shared what he'd stolen; he was a bank robber who loved to tell the story of how he had once given away all his possessions. At the beginning, his way of seeing things left me shaking my head, baffled. "To have all is to have nothing," he'd say, and I'd think, "What is this guy talking about?" But I was drawn to him, and I don't think it's only because I liked anyone who came up with a weird point of view. Seamus was willing to challenge the things most of us valued. He was willing to challenge them in himself, and if you hung around with him long enough you ended up questioning yourself too.

Whether it was cheese or drugs or money, by the time I met Seamus his attitude was, "What good is this if I keep it to myself?" It probably sounds impossible. "Generous convict" must sound like a complete oxymoron. I don't know all the competing forces inside him that made Seamus a robber who argued that material things weren't important. I do know that I hadn't met many people like Seamus: people who could give without resentment, without keeping a strict account of who owed what, without making you pay even for what was supposedly offered freely.

He could take knives right out of my hand. "Whoa, what's the beef here? Is it really worth it?" he'd inquire, and the fire inside me would slowly cool. He could quiet my wildly jiggling leg just by laying his hand on it until I calmed down. When had someone ever touched me for *my* sake, touched to give me something rather than to take it away?

Seamus was doing time for manslaughter. One day he said to me, "I got off easy. In my mind, it was first degree." His eyes were clear, neither bragging nor hiding. "I deserve to be punished," he admitted. I thought of all the times we'd talked about prison and argued back and forth about its purposes. It was one thing to consider whether prison's role was to punish. It was another to take the secret shame, the line beginning "I deserve..." which for most of us had never ended well, and lay it out in the open. I could see Seamus looking off into the distance and I knew that whatever it was, manslaughter or first-degree murder, the thing he'd done that couldn't be undone was right in front of his eyes. "I wish I could take it back," he said finally.

I didn't know it was possible to feel regret and not die of it. In the middle of an abstract conversation you could slip suddenly into the cool water of honesty and not drown. Seamus was saying more than he had to say, more than any court had asked him to and more than most superficial posturing among inmates required. Inside me I felt the stir of an answering thought. Something that had been present but indistinct began to resolve itself into clarity: *Me too. I wish I could take it back too.*

There is nothing quite like the awareness. Like looking at yourself in the mirror for the first time. You let go of the denial and what you have is an understanding so pervasive it seems to fill your whole body. *Holy shit, I did this.* The knowledge is deeper, more physical, more insistent than on the day you did it.

Why would anyone choose that knowledge? Why did Seamus admit more than he had to? Truth is a door, gets you to a place you can't get any other way. With all his reading and thinking, Seamus must have known that. Eventually, long after Seamus, I came to know it too. And I got so I liked challenging other people. Some guy would be trying to make excuses for what he'd done, saying "I couldn't help it, I had to do it."

"Let me get this straight," I'd say to him. "Someone forced you to walk in there, right? Someone forced you to take that gun out. Someone forced you to pull the trigger."

By this time he was either furious with me and ready to quit the conversation or staring at me with a strange expression on his face because I wasn't playing the game. Oh, I *knew* how to play it. I knew how to work out a logic that put all the blame on the other people. If they'd given me that money right away, I wouldn't have had to get rough. If they hadn't been so sure of themselves, I wouldn't have had to show them how powerless they really were. If they hadn't mocked me, I wouldn't have had to punish them. When you're caught up in the game, these causal connections seem so obvious. You don't see that the logic of those excuses actually says more about you than it says about the victims. It says so much about what matters to you, what terrifies you, what you need, what you can't stand to let anyone else know about you.

Moving beyond this logic isn't easy. A lot of guys probably chose to stay where they were, afraid to hold the full weight of the truth, afraid to let themselves feel the remorse. I ended up having more respect for anyone who could face the truth because that was what I wanted to be able to do, too. But facing it is a complex business. Sure, accountability and remorse are the goals, and the truth really can make you free. But too much shame can paralyze you and drive you deeper into darkness. You need to be strong enough, and most people probably need others who can help them figure out how to look, how to understand what they see, and how to go on from there. Once you understand what you've done, what happens next? What do you do with that knowledge?

I knew in a guy at Walpole who'd been doing angry time for thirty years, ever since he'd gotten a natural life sentence for killing a police officer. Greg was his name, and he was always provoking the guards and getting into trouble. One day he got a request from the son of the man he'd killed: the son wanted to come and visit him.

I like to try to picture them sitting across from each other in the cramped visiting room. All these years later, the son said he'd finally been able to forgive Greg for taking his father's life away.

Hearing about it was like learning there was a cure for a disease you'd thought was fatal. It fascinated me, this loosening of the binding rage. Someone had actually said, "The anger stops here. It stops with me." Someone said there's a way to hold on and let go at the same time. No wonder Greg became so much calmer after that day.

Greg's visitor told him he thought thirty years was enough and that Greg ought to be released from prison. This was amazing, but ultimately it meant nothing, because the system didn't care. Greg was going to die in prison whether or not he was forgiven and whether or not this encounter with his victim's son turned him into a calmer man. The truth wasn't going to make *him* free, I sometimes thought bitterly.

Even today, I still think it should have made some difference: the family's wishes, and Greg's changed behavior, ought to have counted for something. But I know what Bobby would say, what Seamus would say, what any of my real friends would say. The truth does matter, whatever the system does or doesn't do. You strive for honesty, and then for peace, not because of what anyone will give you if you achieve it but simply because of what you get for yourself.

Some insights come from looking in the mirror. Someone takes you and holds you up to it and says *there, see?* and all at once you do see.

But it matters who's doing the showing. Your mother can slam you right up to the mirror and you'll see your father's face looking back at you whether you want to or not. You can stare into the cracked glass on the wall of a cell and see the face of a scumbag monster lock him up throw away the key and who cares if he rots in there. You can stand next to a friend and as you watch him watching you, your vision starts to swirl because he sees something you've never seen before. And some days you're by yourself, just splashing cool water on your face, and you happen to catch yourself there in the glass, your expression both so fierce and so supplicating that you don't even know what you're saying to the world when you confront it each day. Some days it's *keep away, don't mess with me,* but other days it's more like *hey, I'm looking for some answers here and if you got some, I just might be ready to listen.*

There are insights you just stumble into, the way a man bushwhacking his way through the tangled woods can suddenly stumble into a clearing he didn't know was there. When I put my life on the line in Lewisburg soon after that conversation with Seamus, I didn't know what new realizations were waiting for me. Hindsight says there was more guiding me toward those insights than I knew at the time. But I wasn't conscious of it when I decided to fight a guy from New York who owed me money. I fought him because I had to. I fought him because I'd lose face if I didn't.

The Corrections officials had sent me to federal prison as a way of saving face, and we were more alike than I wanted to admit. Saving face ranked way up on my own list of priorities, so high that I *would* risk my life for it.

This guy from New York was called Juan. When I met him in the new man's section he seemed straight up, a decent guy who did what he said he would. For most of my time in Lewisburg, we never had a problem. But then he owed me some money for drugs I'd sold him, and he wouldn't pay. When I went to see him, all he said was, "Don't keep pressing me." He had no excuse even though I was actually hoping he'd come up with one. No excuse meant no way out, and we both knew it.

What I have I guard. Truth is, I have less than you think. Truth is, I'll do anything to keep people from seeing that. There is so little left here in this place where they take so much away and where most of us had too much taken away already. All I have is my honor and I will go down with it. Over money? You can't take it with you, but where am I going? Nowhere. So what matters is now. What matters is how they look at you. I will not be weak. I will not be the kind of person you can cheat. I will not be the kind of person you can take from, because I can't afford it. I have no surplus, no luxury of letting anything slide by. Look at me. This is not someone you can dupe. No chump no punk no coward I am someone who will stand his ground. Today is a good day to die. If it comes to that, and it may.

In prison, there was nowhere to run, even if you were tempted to run. There was no real way to walk away calmly, either, because we were all locked up together. In prison, if someone thinks you're a chump he's going to think it every day and you're going to have to walk past him and *see* him thinking it. There's no taking time to cool off, no "let's just steer clear of each other." Even people who were readier than I was to believe that fighting wasn't necessary were still caged with their enemies day after day in a situation more heated, more likely to erupt, than on the street.

So Juan knew I had to fight him; he probably accepted it as inevitable. He might have wondered why I didn't let my friend Bulldog do the fighting, because Bulldog was working for me and he was the one Juan owed the money to directly. But the way I saw it, Bulldog shouldn't be taking the risk. He was getting out in a few months and he had a wife and kids waiting for him, and that added up to more worth living for than I had. My own sentence still stretched out so far I couldn't imagine the ending. And I was still daring life to prove itself to me. I didn't feel like I had much to lose if I died in this fight, but I had a lot to lose if I stayed alive and didn't go through with it.

Fights have a choreography of their own. Juan says "I'll see you tonight in the gym," and when night comes I'm ready. Here's how it works: Bulldog goes to check things out and comes back saying *yeah, he's there*, so I walk into the stairwell with a knife hidden in my sleeve, the blunt piece of steel waiting against my arm. Juan's got his hidden in his glove and as soon as I see him unwrap it I let mine drop down, visible at my wrist. At this signal we move toward each other and the dance begins: my knife at his neck, then his at my ear, and we're in it. The knives do their swift work, slicing our arms as we try to block each other, and then he finds an opening and his blade pierces my chest. I step back to escape the blow but step too far, losing my footing and falling back down the stairs. His advantage, now, and he takes it. All at once he's on top of me, pinning me so my knife looms ready to stab him but I can't move my arm to do it, and his knife is slicing the breath out of me as he thrusts it into my chest once, twice, I can't tell how many times but when I see it arcing up through the air again I know if I don't do something I'll die, and *this is not my time to die*, I know that with a desperate certainty that makes me reach up and grab the blade. It goes right *through* my hand but I hold on, hold on, and he's trying to yank it back from me while Bulldog is trying to take it from me too and I'm saying no, no, I won't give it up, while I hear the air actually hissing from my chest and the pain is starting to choke my awareness until Bulldog says *It's over!* and Juan and his friends are yelling it too and I let Bulldog take the knife from my hand.

It's over, as thoroughly as any storm. With actual courtesy in our voices, Juan and I negotiate: I'll go to the infirmary first and he'll follow in a little while. We won't rat on each other; that's so obvious we don't even have to agree to it. From this point on, if we're asked, we have no idea what happened. The law of honor made us enemies a few minutes ago but now it turns us into allies because this is our business, not theirs.

I can't imagine walking but I'm damned if I'm going to die here in this stairwell, so I let Bulldog help me up and we start crossing the sixty or so yards to the infirmary.

Suddenly here's Seamus, running to catch up with us. "Why didn't you come and get me?" he exclaims as he sees what happened. I look at his funny face and think *Seamus my friend.* I swear I'll never forget the way he looks right now, standing at my side in the middle of this emergency.

We're in front of the infirmary with the guard asking us what we want.

"You fucking moron, he's bleeding!" Seamus yells in disbelief. I listen to Seamus agitate and the physician's assistants argue about how serious the wounds are and then I interrupt because I don't have time for these fine points. "I can't breathe!" I tell them, and finally they spring into action, figuring out what hospital to send me to. It's incredible how long it takes, how much procedure gets in the way, and as it starts to feel like one of those dreams where you can't get where you're going, I wonder if my mind is getting fuzzy or if they're deliberately stalling.

It's a tricky business, trying to save the life of a dangerous man. I'm lying on a gurney, racing toward the trauma unit of the hospital, and in the huddle of doctors yelling rapid instructions to each other is a federal marshal with a machine gun – another crucial member of the team. I'm naked as we speed down the hallway and I'm suddenly conscious that it's a female doctor trying to insert a tube into my groin. I'm embarrassed that she sees this: my nakedness, but also this whole scene, this man who deliberately walked into trouble and made it necessary for her to save him.

Whether I asked for it or not, there were people whose job it was to save people like me. Back in North Carolina, doctors had worked to save a kid who administered his own poison, and now these doctors were working to save me without asking what this felon had done or whether he deserved to live. "Don't you feel this?" the surgeon asked a few minutes later, incredulous because I wasn't screaming in pain even though he was threading a tube into my lung.

"Aren't you here to help me?" I countered. As if it was a natural thing for me to recognize help and accept it. But I *was* ready to let them get me out of this. Even though I'd walked into that stairwell sure that I would take what came, now I was ready to let the doctors bring me back.

The surgeon regarded me with what looked like respect when I told him I could stand the pain because I knew he was helping me. But could I have explained to him that physical pain was often a relief to me? It was so much more concrete and understandable than the emotional kind. At least with an injured body it was clear: this is what hurts, this is why.

When I was finally stabilized, the surgeon sat by the bed and asked me what had happened.

"I got stabbed," I told him matter-of-factly.

"Stabbed," the doctor repeated, confusion and sadness troubling his eyes. Here was prison turned inside out, the guts of it exposed. I watched him try to understand what he saw.

I got back to Lewisburg and something strange was waiting for me there. Slick Jones greeted me by saying, "Hey, I would have paid that money for him," and my mind reeled. What was he talking about?

Slick would have been sorry if I'd died – I knew that's what he was trying to say. Caring, of all things, from Slick at the end of the tier, and it kept coming, too, from other guys who heard I was back: "Hey, Reb, how are you? Are you feeling OK?"

The doctor had felt it too. I saw it suddenly, what the concern in his eyes had been for: me, my life, how close I'd come to losing it.

Whether you're looking in the mirror or out at the rest of the world, what you see is actually, miraculously, up to you. That was the astonishing idea that began to take hold in the days after I got back from the hospital. Am I bad or not? Is life worth living or not? All the years I'd been looking for someone else to tell me, and here I was stumbling over an insight I couldn't believe I'd missed for so long.

It was coming so close to death that did it: when you can actually feel the breath hissing out of you, you start to think that maybe breathing is pretty damn amazing and precious and not so easily squandered. But it wasn't only that. I'd been near dying before and it hadn't left me feeling like this. Saved from amphetamine poisoning at 16, what I noticed most were the scars. The bad luck, the damage, more reasons to curse the unforgiving world. Now at 29 I was returned – not even to the open road but to a locked tier – and it started to seem like there had to be a reason. If I got through that fight alive, there must be something to it. Something I'm here to do or find out or show.

I lay on my bed running my hands over the scars on my body and thinking about what I'd done with all the years of living and breathing I'd been given so far. *Nothing but hurt,* I said to myself, and I let myself think it and know it and not try to make it any prettier than it was. *You've hurt people, you've hurt yourself, and that's all you've done. You almost died, and what would they have written on your tombstone: he left a wake of devastation everywhere he went. Is that what you want?*

I was holding *myself* up to the mirror and taking an inventory, but the extraordinary thing was that as harsh and unsparing as I was being, I wasn't left paralyzed by the shame and the waste. Instead I felt galvanized in a way I could hardly remember ever having felt. It was time to get busy. The business of life is *living.*

A few weeks after I got back from the hospital, Seamus and I were doing angel dust together. Yeah, I was still doing drugs when I could get them. The interesting thing was, something different happened this time. We were sitting there together and the prison walls melted away. I felt them *gone,* and blooming throughout my body was a tingling so sharp it made me want to turn to Seamus and say, "Are you feeling this?" And then in that suddenly wall-less prison what I felt was peace, so deep and abiding and absolute that I didn't think it could be mine to feel on this earth. *I can heal myself, I can create this feeling,* I said as the old shame and fear and fury flew away like released birds.

Maybe the best analogy is Native Americans who use peyote as the catalyst for visions they're meant to have and meant to keep long after the drug has worn off. So often, what you feel when you're high has nothing to do with what you feel later on, but the extraordinary thing was that this peace felt like *mine*, belonging to me rather than to the drug. As the days and weeks went by, I kept checking to see if it was still with me — kind of the opposite of the way you keep checking a toothache to see if the pain is still there — and it was. Not as something that made every moment perfect and free of frustration, but as a reminder, maybe. An almost physical reminder of what I'd been figuring out since I came back from the hospital: that I had what I needed to make things be different from now on.

Nobody wants to hear that drug trips are what really make the difference to an incarcerated man. But to me this incident counts, it stays with me. It was a clearing I stumbled into, but I'd been tearing and thrashing through the brambles for a long time on my own, and maybe I was following blazes on the trees all along without being fully conscious of doing it. Maybe I didn't just stumble; maybe I have to give myself more credit for actively looking.

Ever since 10 Block, I'd worked to cultivate the rage I felt at the prison system. Rage was what I had, what I knew how to use. Without it, I was sure prison would break me. Maybe I'd never have looked for another way if the rage weren't eating me up inside. But it was, and after enough time I couldn't help but feel it. On some level, I must have been wanting more. What was all that reading about, after all? Why did I gravitate toward Seamus, toward Bobby, toward people who seemed to have something else or at least to be striving toward it?

Right in the middle of the amazing moment with Seamus, I probably thought those birds of fury and shame had flown away forever. No movie endings, though: the scene doesn't fade out on a man who was forever afterward peaceful and unclaimed by his old demons. The stabbing and the aftermath of realizations marked a turning point, no question about it. But rather than saying I *found* peace that day, it feels more accurate to say I got a promise of it. A sense that there could be more for me than I'd known, and more worth working for if I bothered to try. Just as having one good meal doesn't stop you from being hungry again the next day, and one empathetic response doesn't keep you from feeling crazy and alone the next time, the peace and the life-affirming moments of Lewisburg didn't inoculate me against future doubt and despair. But now when those demons surfaced, there was something in me that was strong enough to put up a good fight.

Eight years into my prison sentence and it was time to get serious. Time to take this life I'd been given and make it into something I valued. But as a state prisoner in the federal system, I couldn't do much more than bide my time; I wasn't allowed to take classes or participate in programs. I started to realize that if I was going to get serious, Massachusetts was probably the place to do it. I started thinking about how to get back.

Anna's dream was that she would hire a great attorney and find a way to get me out of prison altogether. She'd had this dream for a long time, and whenever she talked about it, I had to remind myself that loving a man in prison isn't easy. Even for Anna, who always claimed she'd hang on no matter what. Another nine or ten years – whatever the final sentence might actually come to – was still a long time to wait.

When she brought up the idea of getting a lawyer, I kept saying, "What's the use? I pled guilty, I *am* guilty – what do we think is going to change that?" But she persisted, and finally I told her there was one thing we could try. A couple of months after my trial, there'd been a change in the law regarding what the judge has to say to the defendant when he asks, "How do you plead?" I thought it was possible I could make a motion to withdraw my guilty plea on this basis. Withdrawing the plea would mean seeking a motion for a new trial, and maybe that would open up possibilities – maybe I'd get a new sentence for which the time I'd already served would be enough.

It was a long shot, but I was trying to find *something* that would do this for her, or for us. She found an attorney who looked over what I'd proposed and said yes, it was possible to argue this.

I didn't tell Anna or this lawyer about the doubt that still nagged at me. In my own head, I tried to argue it out: OK, it's true that I'm guilty. In some ways I'm even guiltier now than I was then, because I get it now, I understand what I've done. But maybe the eight years I've served *are* enough. I've certainly come a hell of a long way already. And Anna's been waiting a long time for me. How long can you really expect a woman to wait? Maybe I'm not sure if I could make it on the outside, but will I be any surer years from now?

I let Anna take out a loan to hire the attorney, and I even let my mother contribute some money, although I ended up regretting that because it only led to trouble. My mother was skeptical of Anna and skeptical of any lawyer she chose, and she ended up embarrassing me in front of both of them by making a fuss and questioning everything.

And then we lost the case, and I wondered if we'd shaken everything up for nothing. I felt like I'd failed Anna, like she'd been urging me toward something I just couldn't do. But I also felt like she'd failed me. She got me all caught up in this crazy scheme that probably never had much chance of working out, and she tried to draw me into her dream of us being a normal couple on the outside, rather than letting me focus on my life where I was. Who could blame her? Her feelings made all the sense in the world. But after we lost, it got harder and harder to look into each other's eyes. That might have been when things started to go bad for us, even though I didn't really cut her off until a couple of years later.

I did find a way to get back to Massachusetts, though – the thing I'd wanted in the first place. After the fight in Lewisburg, I saw that I might be able to use that incident as a way to get back. I could make the case that conditions weren't safe for me in Lewisburg. Maybe it sounds like I was pulling something over on them, manipulating the system to get what I wanted. But it's not as if you can just ask nicely for a transfer, especially not from federal prison back to state. Once you're in the federal system you disappear from the state system unless they decide to let you back or unless you can find some way to get a judge to undo the transfer. Ironically, even my honest reason for wanting to come back – that I wanted access to classes and programs – wouldn't have done it. So I decided to file a case about being at physical risk in Lewisburg even though Anna was also pursuing the motion that might get me out of prison completely. This way, I figured, I'd be covering all the bases, and whatever happened would be better than staying in Lewisburg.

So Anna got all the paperwork ready, and on the day that I was shipped to Massachusetts for the hearing on the motion we'd filed, she filed the other motion about Lewisburg being a danger to me. That got us a temporary injunction to keep me in Massachusetts while we waited for both decisions.

I won the case against Lewisburg before we heard a decision on the other motion, so I knew that I *would* be staying in Massachusetts, at least. And when I lost the other case a few months later and knew I wouldn't be getting out any time soon, that sharpened my desire to buckle down and focus on my life in prison. In a way, it was like the difference between getting out by magic and by working for it. I wasn't going to get sprung by some special legal trick; I was going to have to serve all these remaining days, so I might as well see what I could do with them.

When I first got back to Walpole I was locked up in segregation, same as before. But I figured soon enough even the cops would notice the difference. I stopped making an issue out of everything they said or did, and I went for months without getting a single disciplinary ticket. Finally they figured out I wasn't the threat I'd been a year ago, although it wasn't because federal prison had broken me. It was because I'd decided I had better things to do with my time.

I got let out into the general prison population, where there were classes and programs and more freedom of movement on the tiers than seg allowed. I was figuring out how to make things work in prison, and meanwhile Seamus was on the street figuring out that he didn't know how to be free. I called him sometimes from Walpole, and my call to his house would get forwarded to his cell phone wherever he happened to be. "Guess where I am?" he'd say to me, and I'd take the bait and say "Where?", ready to hear about another Seamus caper.

"I'm standing in the middle of a crack house, and there's another one right across the street – I can see the cops making a raid on it right now –"

He was trying for his usual laughing amazement at the crazy wonders of the world, but the truth is he sounded like a journalist reporting from a war zone, telling you about the bombs falling all around him but clearly unable to do anything to stop them. It was as if he *knew* he was fucking up, knew he wasn't offering any kind of good example, but all he could do was report the news to me. *I'm standing in the middle of a crack house and this is what it's like out here.*

He came to visit that winter, all the way from D.C., arriving with clothes and books and asking what else I wanted. He was still living his paradoxes: I knew it had to be stolen money that bought me those gifts and I knew Seamus still thought nothing was worth having unless you shared it. And were those gifts apologies too, in a way? Was he apologizing for being free while I wasn't, or for being free but actually still being as bound and tethered to his old ways as ever?

Preoccupied with my own struggles, I couldn't really imagine how impossible the street life was turning out to be for Seamus until one of Anna's visits about a year later.

"I've got something really terrible to tell you," she said the moment she sat down.

"Who died?" I asked her, bracing myself.

It was Seamus, of course, Seamus who was probably never made for this world. It was the first time I'd ever cried in front of Anna. All her own tears had never brought me to my own, so I guess you could say Seamus gave us that. After a minute I said to her, "I'm crying for myself. Seamus is probably better off. He's at peace, like he always said he wanted."

I was crying the way the living do, because the dead go off and leave us to figure things out on our own.

They said it was suicide. Seamus had kept an address book of his friends and Anna was listed next to my name, so his sister called her when she was calling everyone who would want to know about Seamus. "They're saying he killed himself," she told Anna, "but we think the FBI killed him." Anna wanted to know what I thought and I said I didn't know. Maybe they were chasing him and he knew he was caught and killed himself to be free. The details didn't really matter to me; I was busy trying to figure out his legacy. Were peace and freedom impossible in this life, after all? Was everything we'd talked about meaningless? Or just wrong?

Mourning him, remembering him, I talked and argued with him in my head. After a while I said, OK, Seamus, go. Go and be free that way. I'll always miss you, but I'm not going to give up on the other way just yet.

So I hung in there, trying for that other way. Signing up for college classes at Walpole showed me that you could come back and go forward, both. When I finally got out of segregation and went down to the school, the first person I saw was Bill, the DOC guy who had told me my GED score years ago and was so excited about getting me into classes. Now he looked up from his papers and smiled when he saw me.

"I'm glad *you're* back! Where've you been?"

"I've been down in 10 Block, I've been to Lewisburg ..."

I've been to hell and back, Bill, that's where I've been. But now I'm here and I want to get going on the rest of my life. He gave me the forms to fill out and I had them back on his desk in only a few minutes. A lot of guys would take the paperwork and then go and think about it for days, weeks, whatever would let them say "Yeah, I'm getting it together, I'm going to school," even if they never showed up for a class. But I slapped those forms down on Bill's desk and he knew I meant it. *Glad you're back.* Me too, Bill, me too.

I chose from a list of classes. When I saw that Christopher Lydon was going to be teaching fiction writing, I knew right away I wanted that one. I'd seen him on the TV news, seen the way he looked people straight in the eye and asked them questions like he really wanted to know. *Tell me who you are,* that's what he always seemed to be asking. I looked at the sign-up sheet and took a deep breath. A writing class with Chris Lydon wasn't going to be any kind of joke. If I took it, I'd be jumping in with both feet. I signed up.

He walked into the first class wearing the most beat-up sneakers I'd ever seen. He sure didn't look like he did on TV. To me those sneakers said *I'm real* and *I'm not afraid of you.* He got right down to business and told us we'd be writing short stories and he hoped we would be able to write two pages a week.

Two pages a week, and his voice is filling the room, soothing like a lullaby. Yeah, like you know what a man sounds like singing a lullaby? Well, if there is such a thing, this is it, but he's waking me up too, he's saying come on, you can do this, we can do it together. Here in a classroom where we're all locked in and the windows are sealed shut and God knows what these men have done. But he's not worried about that, he's here anyway. Behind me some guy is asking do we really have to write two

pages a week and I'm crazy with impatience because he doesn't get it. Here's this
famous man who could do anything and he comes here and does this with us.

People come in smelling of the outside. It's everywhere on them, a
private breeze they bring along. Chris swept in talking about singing in a
choir, reading to his kids at night. If I had the nerve I'd have asked the
questions right back to him: *tell me how you got to be the way you are. Tell me*
how they make men like you.

For me, Chris was the point of the class. I wasn't going to waste time
making excuses about why I couldn't get the work done. Yeah, we all
know there's enough madness on the tier in any week to keep you from
pulling out the notebook and getting busy. But I figured if the Pell
Grants could give us the notebooks and Chris could give us his time, I
could sit on my bed and try to write a story every week.

But what do you say? How do you say it? I was trying to talk to Chris
in those stories but the other guys were listening in, so I held back and
Chris could tell. He wrote "wonderful" and "beautiful" in the margins
but he teased me about ending the stories by killing everyone off. "That's
your favorite literary device: the nuclear flyswatter," he said. He was
right. I'd kill off the characters because it was the easiest way to get out
of it, to close whatever I'd opened. Just as the characters would get a little soft or tender, I'd slam the story shut.

It was because of the other guys in the class. That's why my stories
weren't as honest as they could have been. "Rebel, what are you *talking*
about?" these guys said when I brought up an idea that was too wacky or
too far out – or maybe too close to home. I wanted to be direct with
Chris but there were so many things in the way. He was up against a lot,
trying to get any of us to write for real.

Later, after the class had ended and Chris and I were writing letters,
he told me he was thinking of teaching another class and he asked what
story topics I would suggest he use. I came up with a list that I pretended had nothing to do with me: "The pain I felt the most." "My first
puppy." "Me and my Dad out and about." "Why did you have to die and
leave me alone?" "My pajamas with the feet in them." Each one was a
door to something you couldn't avoid. A guy could go ahead and write
about that first puppy, or he could say to Chris, "Yeah, right, my first
puppy. Except I never had a puppy because my bastard of a father
wouldn't let me have one." Whatever the deal was, at least the writer
would be going after something real.

I was great at making suggestions for other people. Meanwhile, I was still being indirect with Chris. He didn't know that all those topics were doors to my own stories, too. I could have told him that *why did you have to die and leave me alone* was my question to my grandmother, or told him about "the pain I felt the most," or told him how ironic "me and my Dad out and about" was. I could have written the memory of skidding down the hallway in my feet pajamas, Sparky chasing after me in a wild frenzy and neither of us knowing how soon everything was going to change. How Sparky wouldn't come with us when we moved to Florida, how my father wouldn't come with us when we moved back home. How impossible everything about the scene would later feel – both the easy delight of the skidding and the safe thud at the end.

I am writing to say "Hello Chris, I miss you and the feeling of joy your class brought." Writing that first letter was even harder than signing up for the class. He'd come and gone, and I was looking after his retreating back, calling out "Wait! Don't go yet!" Part of me knew he'd keep on walking. Or turn around just for the time it took to say, "What're you, crazy? Did you really think I was *that* interested in you?"

Who knew what men did when they disappeared? They just left, and Chris could too – walk back out the prison walls for the last time and re-enter his world of wine glasses and airplanes and family around the dinner table. But I wrote. I sent those letters out after him and he did write back. Didn't say I was crazy. Didn't say "I've got my own life here and I'm way too busy for you."

Each letter I wrote him felt like I was opening my rib cage a little wider, showing him the soft heart inside. After I sealed the envelope I felt the fear close back around me and I'd think *What did I just do?* I kept waiting for him to say I'd gone too far, he was sick of my childish rambling. When his reply was a long time coming, I was sure he was trying to figure out how to tell me to stop writing. But the reply always came. One time he sent a postcard from his trip to Ireland. Another time he told me he'd quoted from my letter in a commencement address he was giving. And so I answered him, page after page of handwriting on yellow legal paper.

Right away I made a point of spelling out the criminal charges that had landed me in prison. I wanted Chris to have the facts. A teacher coming in to prison looks around the room full of convicts and has no idea what any of them have done. If he starts to like them, starts to think they seem like decent guys, maybe he'll begin to doubt himself or to look for ways around it. He'll tell himself that maybe this one didn't really do it. Maybe the trial was rigged, or maybe he didn't *mean* to do it. If Chris was going to have faith in me, I wanted him to know what he was up against. And I wanted him to know how desperate I was to make something better. My letters told him things I would never have said in class:

It's so wonderful that I saw my words in the Commencement speech. I knew you cared and that is so very important in here. I have others I write, but none I treasure more than you. I say things and then I'm embarrassed ...

I appreciate you being my brother and allowing me to say things and not be ridiculed because of my candor. I am in search of self and since I have had a faulty pool to draw examples from, I have to explore my thoughts and feelings with those I trust and value ... Thank you for tolerating my immature groping for self-awareness.

It is the thought of earning your friendship that propels me towards something beyond me as yet. You renew my spirit that falters so often.

They read like love letters, and in a way they were. Without the detailed sexual longings that my early letters to Anna had, but with longing and fear and wishing of their own. I was throwing bottles overboard into the ocean, and it was easier to do it if I could imagine them caught and held by another person.

But I could only handle the exposure in small doses. When he came to visit one time I was awkward, like I'd stripped naked for him on paper and now had to stand there in front of him with no cover. He tried to hug me goodbye and I froze, wanting to do the right thing but completely out of my element.

I'm going to be a stronger and better human being from this, I wrote. *I no longer want to be a loser in this losing game.* I made these vows, I told Chris about the books I was reading and the picture of a lighthouse on my wall and all the ways I was trying to hold on. The letters are full of promises I was hoping I had the right to make. Chris sent me books, he quoted me in his speech, he did everything he could to let me know what he saw in me. But I don't know if he ever saw the doubt that was also there in every letter: do I even deserve to try to grow something new in such scorched and devastated earth? Sometimes the hardest thing about trying to change is convincing yourself that you're worthy of the effort. That you haven't already blown all the chances any one man gets.

I tried not to tell Chris too much about the tedium and madness of daily life in prison. I didn't want to seem like I was complaining. Better to tell him about the classes I was taking or what I thought of Thoreau's *Walden* or Joseph Campbell's *The Power of Myth* than to whine about what the line officer did that day. But sometimes I couldn't help it. When I got sent to segregation again, I had to tell him, even though I didn't know if he could understand what it meant.

I wasn't sure *I* knew what it meant, this time. After two years in population, two years of classes and letters and the belief that I was finally making something decent of my life in prison, something happened that got me locked up again. They called it encouraging a riot. I called it standing up for a friend who had stood up for me years before. Ron had joined me on the hunger strikes all those times I was trying to make a statement in 10 Block, so now, when I saw seven cops all going after him at once, I didn't think twice about getting in the middle of it.

We were in the yard, about to go back inside, when I saw them up ahead, a tangle of cops and Ron at the center. I yelled to Sean, and the two of us started running, shouting "Leave him the fuck alone!" with a whole crowd of other guys joining in and running with us. It was a sight you don't see every day in prison: two white guys heading the pack of black men rushing to defend another black man who's being jumped. I could hear the cops screaming, "Get back, get back into the yard," and I'm yelling "No, give us Ron!", but then Ron surrendered. "I'm OK," he told us, and the cops – you could see them still shaking from the adrenaline – said, "Harrison, it's over."

They took Ron away to segregation and Sean and I stayed out in the yard, waiting. We knew the minute we walked back in through the door they'd take us away too, so we figured we'd hang on to every last minute of freedom. Up in the control towers, they were watching us with their binoculars, but no one moved until the yard closed and we had to come in. Sure enough, as soon as we crossed the threshold they snapped the cuffs on us and took us to 10 Block.

"I don't really care," I wrote to Chris as I tried to explain to him what had happened. "I don't really care because I helped a friend who was being mistreated." I did feel that way, but I was trying to talk myself into it a little, too. Trying to believe that going to segregation again didn't mean I was backsliding. These are the things that happen in prison but it doesn't mean I'm going to lose everything I've gained these past couple of years. "I'm not going to waste this time," I promised Chris, even though it looked like I was going to get a lot of seg time and that meant no more college courses for a while. "I have a list of books which I call my mind-survival books. And I have math books and a dictionary to carry me through." All these years later, I was still doing that exercise: flip open the dictionary, find a word, try to use it in a sentence.

I couldn't tell Chris this news without immediately telling him not to worry about it. "Don't cry for me," men in prison say to people on the outside, and we say it at least as much for ourselves as for them. We see them looking at us and see the helpless pain in their eyes and know we're just as helpless to fix it. Chris asked me about visiting and I told him not to come because I didn't want him to have to deal with visiting 10 Block. The truth is I didn't want him to see me in chains; I wanted him to keep thinking of me as the man who walked freely to his classroom and wrote stories for him. I wanted to keep thinking of *myself* that way.

In the end, Sean and I were in 10 Block only a couple of weeks before I took a chance and asked if we both could go to 9 Block instead, and we got it. It's always easier to get an internal move than to get moved to another prison or to come back from the feds to state prison. And the cop who was now the lieutenant in 10 Block remembered how Sean and I had made his life hell in the old days; he was probably glad to get rid of us now. Nine Block was still segregation, but it was better than 10 in a lot of ways: there were just bars on the cells, not the isolating steel doors; we exercised in the gym together rather than in separate cages; the visits were contact visits. The food trays still came through the slots in our cell doors, and I still couldn't take any courses. But the atmosphere was less bleak and brutal than 10 Block was, and I was right when I told Chris I knew how to make good use of books by then. So I got through it OK. As it turned out, the biggest surprise of that time wasn't anything that happened on the block. The biggest surprise came from the outside.

I always wondered if Chris's children knew how lucky they were. They stood whole and solid, with no idea how it felt to be as gutted as I was. Years ago I'd told the intake counselor at Walpole that I had no idea if my father was alive or not. I *didn't* know, but for a long time I thought the weight of his silence meant he had to be dead. There was no way you could be that gone and still be alive.

Well, it turns out we believe what we want to believe. What we can bear to believe. The mute indifference of the dead is easier than the mercilessness of a father who *could* call but just doesn't bother. So when he turned up alive, twenty-two years after his last phone call to me, I took that news and spun it the way I needed to: this must be what I've been waiting for all this time. He's come back, he's made the call.

It wasn't his voice on the phone after so long. No, it was his 13-year-old daughter who found us: another kid hungry for the missing pieces. Curious about the other kids she heard were out there somewhere, she called every Harrison in North Carolina until she found my brother. She told Joe she was his half-sister and he had a half-brother too and a father who was alive after all. Alive but once again leaving his family.

Joe was suspicious. He wondered what this kid wanted from us. I wanted to shake him through the phone wires when he told me: didn't he get it? She wanted us because she wanted him, anything of him. She wanted us so she could understand him better. She wanted us because maybe we would be her family. Oh, I got it, I understood her exactly; I could have thrown my arms around this searching kid.

This wasn't how I'd pictured it happening, but once I heard about it I decided it made sense. This girl finds us and it's like she's reaching out to the boy I was. Yes, it fits. For all I know, he asked her to call and look for us. Maybe he admitted to her that he had these boys out there that he missed and she said, "I'll find them, Dad ..."

See what we create when we want something badly enough? All those years I told myself I didn't care anymore, would just spit on his grave if I ever found it, and then when the time came, I discovered that I would take the tiniest scrap of promise and hallucinate a feast. When I wrote to Chris the day after I heard the news from Joe, I wrote as if the forgiving and the healing were a done deal. *This is going to be it, Chris; this is what will make a difference for me.* I was already planning how I'd talk to my father on the phone, how he'd come to visit me in prison, how his new kids would become my family.

I took this hope and ran with it. Ran so headlong into the scene that I hardly stopped to notice I'd way overshot the target. In my head I'd already reconciled with him and was deciding how to break the news to my mother. Joe was wary of telling Mom too; at least we saw that part of it the same way. I knew she was going to come between me and my father again, mock me for wanting him, make me have to defend him. But I had vindication now. *Mom, he must be sorry ... see how he found us again ...*

What jolted me out of my illusions was that my mother *wasn't* furious. She was even more ready to be seduced by him than I was. It was as if there was only so much belief and hope to go around, and as I watched her teeter on the edge, ready to fall for him again, I started to see what fake magic we were all about to believe in. He traveled across the country to see her, retraced his steps back to North Carolina. What did she think – that she could go back and be 16 again and get it right this time? Joe told me he'd seen them together, holding hands. Damn, this guy knew how to work people. But he'd left us before, and now he'd left another family. What were the odds he'd stay with my mother this time if she really decided to throw away her life with Grady and take my father back?

I'd wanted my father for so long that I didn't know what it was like to be a man without that twisted, choking hunger. The loss was in me; it had formed me. But it feels as if it wasn't until that day in prison, 22 years later, that I finally saw it clear and true. I used to know loss through drugs or lust or fury – all those frantic attempts to fill it. Now I just sat there with it and didn't call it any name except its own: he did this. He did this to me, to all of us.

Yes, it was something like realizing what I had done myself. It was the same kind of honesty, the same attempt to hold the full weight of it in my hands. And so when I finally did speak to my father on the telephone from prison, I left no room for illusion. I didn't cut him any slack at all.

"How many mailboxes have you walked by in the past 22 years? How many phones?"

I listened to him fumbling for excuses and I was already shaking my head because I could tell he wasn't going to own up to anything.

"I had a new family," he was saying. "I'd left the past behind –"

"You're fucking right you did. You left *me* behind."

He was a coward. More than anything else, that's what he was. He couldn't look himself straight in the eye and see his failures staring back at him. He couldn't look at his son, his grown man son with the big empty space where a father should have been, and just admit it, just fucking *admit* that yes, he did this. *I may be a jailbird,* I said to myself that day, *but I'm more of a man than he is because at least I know what I've done.*

I knew what I'd done and I knew now what I'd lost. Both were irretrievable. If I was going to move forward it was going to have to be by finding a way to bear those losses, not by pretending I could fill them with anything except the truth. My half-sister didn't stay in touch after finding us; I don't know if she'd had enough of us or nowhere near enough to be satisfied, but either way, we didn't become each other's new and better family. I don't know if my father ever fully realized what he'd done. My mother didn't take him back after all. She snapped out of it too and realized Grady was the one who had been there all those years. She realized, I guess, that she couldn't have herself at 16 again, any more than I could have myself at 12 returned to me and made whole. She stayed with Grady right up until she died, a year after I got out of prison.

And two years after that, my father turned up again, but this time he really was dead. He died by himself in a VA hospital a couple of thousand miles from me. I filled out the forms to bury him, wrote "son" where it asked about relation to the deceased, and wondered what that word could mean if it described 30 years of absence.

It should have meant his death didn't hurt me, but emptiness has its own brutal power. Both their ghosts came to haunt me that April of his faraway death. My father's came saying *now this will never be fixed,* and my mother's came saying *You're just like your father,* just the way she'd said so many times when she was alive.

I'd come so far by then. I was doing so well and still I almost gave them both what I thought they wanted. *Fuck it all, I'll just become him and be done with it. I'll stop trying so hard to turn things around and do it different.* Maybe it would have been a relief, in a way, to give in to that. Like the relief of getting caught by the cops at age 21, because I could just stop even trying to outrun it.

If my father had come to visit me in prison, would he even have recognized my face? If I had visited him in the hospital before he died, he might not even have known me.

Does it matter?

Yes, it does. The loss is mine, the loss is his. Now and always.

No, it doesn't matter, because when I look in the mirror I know who I'm seeing and it isn't only him. It isn't only me-missing-him.

It was a hard and fragile season after his death, but I did find solid ground again. And kept walking.

You go to the king; he doesn't come to you. That's why anyone who wants to talk to Bobby goes to his cell, not the other way around. He stands there making coffee in his hot pot and he always offers me a cup. I hang around drinking it and looking at his books. Just like I hung around Seamus's cell in Lewisburg, looking. Not knowing exactly what I'm looking for. Hoping the other guy will be able to figure it out.

A cop comes by and says "You can't be in there." If it were up to me, I'd explode at him, ask him what the fuck it matters if I'm in this cell or my own. But this is Bobby's territory, so I look over at him. He doesn't have to say anything. I see it in his eyes, in the stillness of his body as he crosses his arms and waits. *Chill out,* he's telling me. Think a minute. It's only significant if you let it be.

Again, like Seamus. Quieting me, making me evaluate it: is it worth it, is it worth it? Do you have to get crazy and worked up over *everything?*

I leave the cell, walking past the cop without even looking at him. I know I'll wait it out and come back the second he's gone.

It looked like compliance, just going ahead and leaving like that. But was it? The thing to understand about Bobby is that he never complied, no matter what it might have seemed like they were doing to him. You could watch Bobby being led down the tier in cuffs and chains and there would always be a look in his eyes that said *there is something in me you can never take away.* Sent to prison just before JFK was assassinated and still here in the late '80s, Bobby had spent more than half his life in prison, but he never really accepted it. Not in the sense of becoming what they wanted him to become. Not in the sense of letting them own him. He was in their custody, but Bobby never belonged to anyone but himself. And he didn't have to keep proving it. He didn't have to hang on to the food tray because even when he let them take it, Bobby never really, actually, gave anything up.

Six years after he had urged me to take the GED, we were together again, on the same block in Walpole. Bobby was working at the prison school and finishing up his college degree and I was cleaning the showers on the block but also going down to the school myself, taking those classes Bobby had talked about back when we first met. I wondered how much he remembered about me, how much potential he still thought I had. Sometimes when I hung out with him I could feel him sizing me up. When he said, "You want to work out?" I knew he had made some kind of decision. He was going to offer me more than coffee, do something more with me than sit around chewing bubble gum and watching TV.

If you measured toughness by how many fights a guy got into, Bobby wouldn't have seemed tough at all. If you measured it by how well he *could* fight, you'd understand why everyone respected Bobby. Anyone who'd done time with him knew he was a solid stand-up guy, well-trained in martial arts, a guy who fought when it mattered. If Bobby had gone 25 years in prison without getting stabbed, it wasn't because he was a chump. It was because he never let anyone make him a chump and he could stop it way before it ever got that far.

It was all in the knowing how, the understanding. The harnessing of one's power. That's why he loved martial arts – it was so much about focus and ability and control. When he said, "I'll teach you some moves," I knew I was lucky, but I was wary, too. What would it be like? You can sit around bullshitting all day with guys who never push you any farther, and then someone comes along and calls your bluff and says OK, if you want this, let's see you work for it. The way Chris said, "Do you want to learn to write?" And there I was with both of them, right at the edge, having to admit they had something to teach me.

What if I couldn't do it? What if I wasn't the fighter I wanted to believe I was? And then the key question, the one I thought of when I pictured the hand-to-hand combat, that same question I could have asked Chris or Anna or anyone who had ever started to matter to me: how close will I have to get?

There was a little open space by the showers, just an area about ten feet by fifteen, and we could stand there and Bobby would show me the moves. Other guys would walk by and see us and sometimes Bobby let one of them join in, but mostly it was just the two of us. Me learning the blocks, the positions, the new way of understanding energy and power.

So you think you're tough? he says. Keep this up for four hours, no, five, and see how tough you feel then. See if you can sustain it. And one day he offers me some grass and I take it like I took the coffee and the bubble gum. I don't guess that Bobby's got a plan here. A lesson. When I'm good and high he says, "OK, let's work out."

"Come on, I don't feel like it."

"Let's do it," he says, and there's no way to argue. He prods me up, he makes me take the stance, and in a minute he's nailed me. I have no focus, no concentration at all. I'm on the ground thinking what a dirty trick this was but when I look at him there's no malice in his eyes. All he's doing is holding me up to the truth. If I don't like it, if I can't stay there long enough to look at it, that's not his fault. The truth is, on drugs you're nowhere near as strong. Anything can happen and you can't count on being able to save yourself.

So you think you're tough? OK, maybe not. I lay there on the ground with him shaking his head at me because I was so wrong about so many things, so misguided, I needed so many lessons. But there was something else in his expression too. How was it I could tell, how did I know that he was also saying *with a lot of work, you could really be something, kid.*

So you think you're tough? Hey, he says, there's nothing so special about rage. Any one of us can get that kind of angry. Any one of us probably already has. The question is, what are you going to do with it?
What are you going to do with it?

He was giving me everything I needed to be the best criminal out there. I would know all that he knew: how to take another person's power and use it for myself. I would be able to block any blow, defuse any strike, destroy whatever enemy I met. If that was what I wanted.

I was always asking questions. "Why should I move my arm this way and not that way?" Always trying to make him justify what he was having me do. Watch, he would say. Just do it. You'll see. He must have known the questions were a way of avoiding the lesson. Avoiding really giving in and learning it. I was resisting it, the way a muscle tenses up and tries to protect itself by getting even tighter. Wasn't that exactly what I'd always done? Ease into it, Bobby would say. Stretch.
The tightness was fear, the way it always is. Fear of pain, fear of contact, fear of giving in and yielding. And what else? Fear of admitting how much I'd been wanting this, and for how long. Bobby must have known that too: the toughest kids are really the most desperate. He must have known what I was really trying to say: teach me how. Stand next to me the way an older man should stand next to a younger one, and show me the way.

I'm stretching my hamstring, and just when I feel like I'm going to break apart because I can't stretch any farther, Bobby says, "OK, where are you right now?"

"I'm at the limit – it's going to snap – I can't do any more."

"All right," he says calmly. "Stay there. Now embrace it. Feel it. Breathe. Then push all the way into that feeling until you're through it."

Right up to the tightness, that's where we'd go each day. To the limit, the impossible pain, the place where I can't stretch any more, but then the breathing, breathing all the way through it, and I am doing it I am not breaking – and suddenly there I am. On the other side. Where the pain is not exactly *gone*, but all right. I can bear it now.

Not under or around, but through. The one option I'd forgotten about, getting me to a place I didn't know I could go. It's not the same as numbing, because when you numb the pain it still owns you. It can grab you again, any time. This way, it's yours. You feel it, you know it, you can carry it. And somehow feel like you're flying.

He was teaching me to take chaotic rage and make something precise out of it. And then what?

Right. And then what. What do you do with what you have, with what you are. Do you think someone's going to *tell* you what to do? Is that what you think this lesson is all about?

Here was the judge's question, still with me. Even after all that had happened, still there was a part of me thinking that one of these days I would find out which of the judge's pronouncements was right. Beyond rehabilitation, or not? Which I is *I*? But here was Bobby staring at me hard and fierce and saying don't you get it? The judge didn't know. There isn't any one of us who knows what you'll do when you get out, except you. So stop waiting to be told if you're bad or good, strong or weak. What does being a man mean? Well, what the fuck do you *want* it to mean, my friend? Who are you going to be in this world? I can teach you anything, but you're the one who's gonna run with it, so figure it out. Decide.

Bobby got transferred to Old Colony, so the martial arts lessons stopped. Some time after, I ended up at Old Colony myself. I had the idea a transfer was coming, because at my classification review hearings they were finally saying I didn't need to be in a maximum security facility anymore. For ten years of review hearings I hadn't been able to shake that classification, and now they were finally lowering it. So they saw I wasn't the man they'd sent to 10 Block all that time ago. But the thing is, I knew that was true no matter what cell they put me in. And I knew I hadn't changed for them, I'd changed for myself. So I wasn't as interested in what they said about me, or where they sent me.

Still, the transfer was going to happen, so when they asked which prison I requested, I said Gardner (the memory of that one amazing week was still vivid in my mind). But the paperwork came back from the Commissioner saying I was going to Old Colony, a new prison within the Bridgewater complex. Old Colony Correctional Center was classified as medium, but we heard it had outside walls and controlled internal movement like Walpole's. Why bother with a transfer, I wondered, if it's going to be just like it is here. But you couldn't get to minimum without going through medium first, and I did want to get to minimum some day. Plus, I knew Bobby was at Old Colony. So I settled into the idea and figured I'd see what this new place would bring.

When I got there I saw that Bobby had already found a place for himself. He was working at the library, and as soon as I arrived he offered me a job there with him. "You'll have all these books to yourself," he teased me, because he knew I'd like that idea. But I was thinking of something else too. It was probably smart to get used to the idea of getting up and going to work every day. The time might come when I'd be glad I'd developed the habit.

So I joined Bobby and Christine, the staff librarian, and learned how to check books in and out, how to catalog them, how to fix them when they got damaged. Regular wear and tear was normal, but if Bobby saw that a guy had deliberately ripped or defaced a book, he let him have it: "What do you think you're doing? These are *our* books."

He meant all of ours. Bobby had always said, "We're all in the same bucket of shit," and this was the same philosophy. We've all got con numbers and we all have to walk when the screws tell us to walk. But if there are any tools here, they're here for everyone. Use them or don't use them, but don't get in someone else's way while you're deciding.

At tables in the middle of the room, men sit reading the newspapers. But look closely: some of them aren't reading at all. They're thumbing the pages, trying to look absorbed, glancing around the room every few minutes to see if anyone is watching. The truth is they're not reading. The truth is they don't know how.

Are any of them ever going to admit it? The way Danny admitted it to me years ago?

I look at them and think of the book under my pillow. The letters I write, the dictionary I use. I think of Danny, stupidly dead. But all those days deciphering newspapers, and the laugh in his voice that time he read the article before I did ...

"Christine," I say, when the other guys have left. "We need to get some easy books, books a guy who can't really read can still figure out. And we need to put them on the low shelves over here, so they're easy to steal."

Christine looks at me. "Why do they need to steal them? Why can't they just check them out?"

I try to tell her about pride. How these guys would rather stare blankly at the newsprint than admit anything to anybody. How stealing is what they know how to do, and how much easier it is than asking, easier than believing they have the right to anything. Don't make them strip naked for you, Christine. Give them some cover, some way to slip those books back to their cells. You'll see. They'll do it.

She believed me. We ordered simple books and left them on the low shelves without making any kind of announcement about it. Sure enough, they started to disappear. After a while, we let them know we knew what they were doing, but we also let them know it was OK. "Listen," Bobby said to new guys who came for orientation. "If you take a book, just leave it on the table in the block when you're done. We'll come get it." So we figured out how to get the books back and no one had to look anyone in the eye. But one day a guy came right up to the desk with his book. He put it down and I glanced at it. A really easy book, a really big tough guy.

"This the first book you ever read yourself?"

"Yeah," he said, and he couldn't help smiling.

"Good for you," I told him, meeting his smile straight on.

Christine gave me and Bobby lists of books and told us to mark the

ones that looked interesting. We always picked current science and tech-
nology books, and we tried to get popular authors, biographies, stuff
people were likely to read. We got all the daily papers and magazines like
Time, Newsweek, Popular Mechanics. And then we liked to give Christine a
hard time.

"Hey, can we get *Playboy? Penthouse?*"

"Over my dead body," she always said. But she smiled saying it.

"OK, how about *Gay Men's World?*"

"Will you stop it!"

We pushed her because we knew she liked us and because we knew
she didn't really mind. She wasn't so afraid of being a woman in a man's
prison that she couldn't take a little ribbing. And she knew how to keep
the teasing light. On Mondays we loved to ask about her weekend, hoping for a good story. She'd smile right back at us and say, "Why should I
tell you? What good does it do you?"

We imagined it would do us a lot of good. "We can live through you,
Christine," we said, trying to draw the details out of her, but she knew
better. A little flirting let us feel like men; too many real details about
Christine's outside life and our loneliness would threaten to rise up and
choke us. You think you want all those vicarious stories, think you'll just
take them and turn them into fantasy later on. But the way they slip
through your fingers like phantoms, the way they are not and can never
be solid – if we kept it going, the teasing would turn to torment, and
Christine was careful never to let that happen. She knew where to draw
the lines with us, not just for her own protection but for ours too.

It's true: there was only so much I could handle. I didn't talk about
Anna – her death just a few months earlier was still so fresh and raw that
I couldn't think about it without turning instantly away. I just savored
those days in the library, joking with Christine, working together with
Bobby, feeling like there was actually some real life worth getting up for
every morning. Some real life, and some small windows: the posters that
came in the mail for new books, which Bobby tacked up on the wall to
make us look like a regular library. The cookies Christine put out at
Christmas. The look on a man's face when he read a book for the first
time. When there is no actual window facing the outside, what you do is
you draw one. You create it, your own frame of possibility, and place it
right in the center of the blank wall.

I worked at the library several hours a day. After I had been at Old Colony a while, I looked into taking college courses again too. The school there was basically like the one at Walpole, but they had an inmate handling the registration, and he recommended Allan Hunter's Shakespeare course. "You sure?" I asked him. I knew I needed the English credit for my degree, but I assumed Shakespeare would be boring. "Yeah, Hunter's really good," Louie said. "But be prepared – you're gonna do a lot of work."

Shakespeare to convicts? Once we got started, I saw that the idea wasn't such a bad one. The plays had it all: murder, deception, intrigue, treachery. Hunter went about it analytically, showing us how the plays worked, how the ideas were still relevant. He had us read aloud in class, and if we felt awkward at first, we got over it. If a guy mispronounced a word, Hunter corrected him, but easily, matter-of-factly. No one ever laughed. We didn't laugh at each other's papers either, but we weren't afraid to say "you're nuts" if the ideas didn't make sense.

Sometimes Hunter himself would read aloud, his English accent so much more Shakespearean than ours, and when I stopped worrying about whether I was smart enough to understand it, I let the rhythm of the language flow over me – all those amazing words, so striking because they were everything I had never felt myself to be: perfectly chosen, perfectly made.

The other thing I learned how to do at Old Colony was teach.

"Look at this," Bobby said, throwing a pamphlet over to me. "This is going to devastate our country." It was a pamphlet about AIDS, and Bobby had a whole stack of information like it. He'd been collecting it for a long time, and he was especially worried about what AIDS was going to mean for guys in prison. Just what we need, he said – something else to isolate us, mark us. Something else to run rampant through the system.

At orientation they showed new prisoners a film about AIDS, but Bobby thought they could do a lot better. This film was so brief it hardly told you anything, and it didn't give the men a chance to ask their own questions. "We need something like a class, something where we can lay it all out in language they're going to understand," Bobby kept saying to me.

Finally he took his idea to the administration, and it turned out they were thinking the same thing themselves – a more comprehensive AIDS program would be a good idea. But it had never occurred to them to have an inmate do the teaching. Bobby was persuasive, and they agreed to let him try it.

He went about it the way he went about everything: thoroughly. He sent away for material from the AIDS Action Committee and then rewrote it in simpler language. He planned how he would get all the information across. He had a way of guessing what the guys were probably wondering about, but he also made sure that they knew it was OK to ask. "There's no question that's a stupid question," he announced during the first class. Then he began to lay out the facts, and I saw the men listening intently. Some of them were there only because of the "good time" (time off their sentence) they'd get for attending, but you could see them start to pay attention in spite of themselves. And even the ones who didn't dare raise their hands in class would come up to Bobby afterwards and whisper, "So, what're you saying? If I let somebody give me a blow job, could I get AIDS?"

Bobby never flinched. He told them to use a barrier, let them laugh when he suggested plastic bags but made sure they got the point anyway. Of course, they'd have to steal the plastic bags from the kitchen – even a prison enlightened enough to offer AIDS classes wasn't going to go so far as to give out condoms and acknowledge that inmate sex was real. Bobby had no patience for denial, and so information about those makeshift condoms was a standard part of his rap.

"Come on, I'll be right there. You can do it."

Now Bobby wanted me to teach the class myself. "I can't teach all of 'em, you've got to help me," he said, grinning.

Get up there and talk about AIDS? Say *blow job* and *condom* and *bodily fluids* to a group of guys? Will I look like I don't know what I'm talking about? Or will I look like I know too much?

But I let him talk me into it. I studied the material, had Bobby quiz me on it over and over. Alone in my cell I stood in front of the mirror and practiced saying the words.

The day came. Bobby sat in the corner like any supervisor watching the student teacher lead his first class, and I started talking. Every time I explained a concept I looked over at him to make sure I'd gotten it right. He nodded his head, a simple *of course* that kept me on my feet and talking. Nobody laughed.

"How'd I do?" I asked him after everyone else had gone. He was smiling in a way that said, come on, you *know* the answer to that one. I looked at the pleasure in his face, felt my own giddy relief, and I realized I did know. I'd been great. "When can I teach the next one?" I asked, and I couldn't stop smiling either.

I taught another class too. Debate class, you might have called it. Or maybe Cellblock Philosophy. Dave and I ran it together.

I'd known Dave back in Walpole, but I'd never really sat down to talk with him. He was a Marine, fought in Vietnam, got wounded twice in combat, and soon after he came home he was facing a murder charge for a killing he said he didn't do. By the time I was on the block with him at Old Colony, he was 20 years into a natural life sentence and still saying he hadn't done it.

In prison you get to be very good at figuring out who's lying to you. Rapists – *skinners*, we called them – said they were innocent or tried to make you think they were in for armed robbery instead. But they changed the story each time, and they could never look you in the eye. Dave, looking right at me, saying "I'm here for something I didn't do" without any bravado, was a guy I was likely to believe. We had a lot of time alone together, time when he could have slipped or decided to come clean, but his story was always simple and always the same.

What got me was how calm he was about it. "Look," he said. "I killed people in Vietnam, so maybe *that's* what I'm doing this time for."

I guess twenty years can make you bitter or philosophical, and by the time I knew Dave he'd chosen philosophical. We sat around in our underwear talking for hours, me crouching on the cell locker and Dave sitting on the bed with a pillow propped up behind him, looking as thoughtful and scholarly as it's possible to look against cellblock walls.

"You know, I was thinking ..." I start out.

Dave smiles and catches the ball I've thrown him. "Well, I've thought about that a lot myself," he answers, and we're off, tossing the day's question back and forth. Are rules necessary? Is the world orderly or chaotic? No question is too big or too weird for either of us. When Dave really gets into it he leaps off the bed and bounces on tip-toes like a boxer while he paces back and forth, going "no, no, no" while I argue "yes, yes, yes" right back at him. We take turns pacing, each yielding to the other's ideas.

Guys on the block walk by Dave's cell, stop, look inside to see what the hell's going on. They can't figure out what kind of show they're watching. Dave and I are going at each other loudly but we're grinning, tossing the balls faster and faster, loving it. Five or six guys crowd in at once, trying to listen. Some don't stay long, just shake their heads and leave, but some get to be regulars. They show up every day to watch the debate, sometimes throwing in a comment of their own. If a guy's just being stupid, trying to distract us, we jump all over the comment and tell him it doesn't make sense. But if he actually has a good point, we grab it and throw it into the air with the rest.

Cops walk by on their rounds and see us crammed into the cell. "Bunch of fucking maggots," I hear one of them mutter. I look at Dave. He's busy making a point and I could swear I see his words streaking through the air, a blaze of color and light in this colorless place. *Maggots?* I think as I turn to look at the cop retreating down the tier. You have no idea what we are.

When I wasn't working with Bobby in the library or debating ideas with Dave, I tried to spend time with Sean. He wasn't on my block so I had to count on seeing him during yard time.

I shouldn't have been seeing him at all. He'd gotten out of prison a few months before but now he was back, keeping to himself and not saying much to anybody. I didn't want him to end up lying on the bed staring at the ceiling the way he'd done when I first met him. There was always the risk, with Sean, that shame would make him give up and forget that life could ever be any other way. So I kept it practical. The first thing I said when I saw him was, "OK, what do you need from the canteen?" Stay matter-of-fact, that was my plan. Don't act like this is any kind of big failure. He knew me too well, though. He said he didn't need anything from the canteen and his eyes told me he knew what I was trying to do. So I got right to the point.

"It's not over, Sean. It's a short sentence. You've done it before and you can do it again."

I tried to kick him back into the ring, make him fight another round, the way Bobby always did to me. Who else would do it for us if we didn't do it for each other?

I didn't ask how he could have been stupid enough to blow his chance. It'd been close to thirteen years since I'd seen the street myself. What did I know about what it took to make it out there?

But the fact is I needed to know. I needed to understand what had gone wrong for Sean, for all the guys I saw coming back. We knew what we hated here. We could sit for hours complaining about it, dreaming of what we'd do if we only had a chance at the door. But what was it about the street that no one could really explain to you, what was it that made it so much harder than it looked, what gave the eyes of the returning men a look of relief mixed in with the shame?

One day in the yard with Sean I finally asked him: "What happened?" He knew what I meant, but he didn't answer right away. I looked around at the men playing basketball, the others standing around in their own little clusters of talk. I waited. Finally he said,

"I just felt like I didn't belong out there."

I felt like I didn't belong out there. It was an answer that covered everything, and it seemed worse than anything he could have said about drinking or drugs or how hard it was to get a job. I thought of my mother visiting me in Norfolk years ago and the way she'd said *you don't belong in here,* almost begging me to agree with her. But I hadn't agreed. I told her this was exactly where I did fit in. Here and not there, with these people and not with anyone else, not for a long time and who knows, maybe not ever again. Wasn't this what Sean was saying now? But I couldn't let it go so easily. Was this really the only place for people like me and Sean? If I got out, would I last any longer on the street than he did?

I realized Sean was still talking. He wanted to tell me more about it, now that he'd started. It turned out all those other things *were* part of it – too much alcohol, not enough job skills, no experience doing anything he could admit to. But I could see it was all the same thing, really – feeling like an alien in the world and even just in your own skin, hating that feeling, not knowing what to do about it, realizing that inside prison or out, the doors to some other kind of life were as locked as they'd ever been.

By the time we finished talking I was convinced all over again that I was doing the right thing by working in the library and continuing to take college courses. At least I'd be as prepared as I could; I was designing my own pre-release program because no one else was designing it for me. Talking with Sean got me motivated, but it also got me angry that we had to figure all this out for ourselves. Did they *want* us to keep coming back? Did it make sense to keep dumping men from medium and even maximum security prisons onto the street with less and less preparation? Was everyone just waiting for us to prove how impossible the odds were?

What happened, I'd asked Sean. If you keep asking it, the question turns into *how* did it happen, what does it mean that it happened, why are things the way they are. And you can ask it about anything. My college classes were teaching me this, how to look for cause and effect, pry open an event and look inside it and try to understand how the guts of it fit together. If it was bad to come out still craving drugs and without a degree or enough skills to get a job, maybe it was also dangerous to come out without enough understanding of how you'd gotten to where you were.

I'd never forgotten what it felt like to tell Sean about the night the man gave me a ride home from the gas station. We never talked about it after that one time, but I knew he knew. All I'd done that first time was say it to him: this is what happened, this is what I never told anybody before. And even then I felt like the world would split open and re-form itself, just because I'd told this untellable thing. Now I decided to take it out again and look at it, really look at it. We were in the yard again, walking around the outer edge where no one would bother us. I brought it up – "You know the time I told you –" and then I got quiet and thoughtful. I could hear the gravel crunching under our feet and I was back in Winston-Salem, feeling myself jump on the bike, hearing the gravel crunching then too, the sound of a boy trying to make his way home.

"Maybe that's why I got so violent later on," I said to Sean. "Maybe that's why I always had to defend my manhood –"

He let me take my time with it, each idea a possible artifact I stuck my hands into the muck and retrieved. "That makes sense," he said finally, nodding his head.

Sense, meaning, some order out of the chaos I'd carried inside me. It was only a beginning, of course. I had these long-buried things in my hands, still covered with crust and mud; I was only just learning to identify them. I was years away from telling anybody the whole story, all the way through and with feeling. But my eyes were open. Tentative, yes, and still scared of these things I was excavating, I was keeping my gaze steady and looking.

The last time Sean had gotten out of prison, before this latest return to Old Colony, the cop who walked him to the door had sent him off with the words, "See you when you get back." The vote of no-confidence was so familiar that Sean hardly even blinked. He'd been in and out of prison for as long as he could remember, and on some level he must have expected to fulfill that prophecy as much as the cop expected him to fulfill it.

So easy and familiar, the business of matching yourself to the world's expectations, matching yourself to the worst ideas anyone has about you. But if you believe you've changed? Believe you're no longer beyond hope? You lie in bed at night staring at the darkness and imagining you feel it, the change that all these years have brought. You breathe in and out and listen to the voice in your head saying *I'm not the same as when I went in, I know I'm not,* and you tell yourself it doesn't matter if anyone else sees or knows.

The trouble was, it *did* matter – not only because other people's lack of faith was so demoralizing but also because there were real, practical ramifications when people in power refused to believe a prisoner had truly changed. "It's just bullshit," the superintendent at Old Colony said about my work at the library, about the AIDS classes, about the college courses I was taking. "You're just hiding your old tricks." Before becoming superintendent here, he'd been a lieutenant at Walpole, and in his mind I was forever the guy who had started the riot, the hard-ass who resisted the cops in 10 Block. That was what was real. That was what he would punish me for.

By this time I'd been at Old Colony almost three years. I *knew* all the work I was doing wasn't bullshit. I figured it was even helping me prepare for freedom, but meanwhile Old Colony was still a medium security prison. I was starting to be able to picture the end of my sentence, and it seemed like I should be getting ready by working my way down to a minimum security and then to a prerelease facility, the way you were theoretically supposed to do. It seemed like it was time to move me somewhere else. And since Bobby and Sean had both been transferred and weren't at Old Colony anymore, I felt as if I had even less reason to stay.

I asked the superintendent about it. "Nothing," he told me. "As long as I'm running this place, you get nothing." No lowering of classification, no hope of moving someplace less secure. So here was another thing that worked one way in theory but in practice was really about whatever the cops wanted to do. "I don't give a shit what you do," the super-intendent added, making it clear that there was no additional program I could enroll in that would make any kind of difference. "You're going to wrap up behind the wall."

That was the last time I tried talking to him about it. I got it: in his eyes I was a fuck-up and always would be. He made me feel like nothing had changed since Walpole – not me, not them, not any of it.

How can you know whether someone has truly changed? How do you know whether to believe it, or trust it? When I'd come back from Lewisburg, *those* officials had seen the difference. They'd let me out of segregation, let the difference actually mean something. They may not have known how it happened, but they took it for what it appeared to be and they let me out so I could start taking classes and working. And over the years there'd been people who believed in change even before they actually saw it: Bobby telling me to take the GED when it wasn't any-where in my mind, the warden at Gardner who decided to treat me as though I was already capable of something different.

But this superintendent at Old Colony had made up his mind about me years ago, and now he was going to make me pay for what I'd done to his officers back at Walpole. He was so fixed on the idea of getting back at me that he was ready to let a man who'd done hard time for years be released directly from a medium security prison to the street. So pre-occupied with the business of settling an old score that he couldn't see anything else.

This standoff we were in was so familiar to me, it tapped something so old and deep, that before I knew it I was steeling myself against him in my mind: *OK, I don't want anything from you anyway. I don't want any part of what you have.* It made me crazy to think that you could scrabble and climb for so long, trying to work your way out of a pit, and just as you got close, a guy with power could stare down at you and say, "Tough shit, you're staying right where you are."

Talking back to him in my mind, I was really trying to talk back to the doubt, too. Trying not to get paralyzed by the thought that maybe I wasn't ready, would never be ready, I'd only been fooling myself all this time. Some days in prison, hope and faith are a lot more fragile than you like to admit. You want to believe you can maintain them on your own, but the truth is, other people do matter. When you look into other peo-ple's eyes, it matters how you see yourself reflected there.

Dealing with the superintendent made me tired, and it narrowed my vision. Everything seemed to be about the struggle he and I were stuck in. When one of the social workers started talking to me about the new drug program Old Colony was starting, I wasn't interested. "It might help you lower your classification," she told me, as if that would convince me to try it. But I already knew that wasn't true. *Nothing, as long as I'm running this place you get nothing.* She was dreaming if she thought anyone could talk the superintendent out of that vow.

I couldn't see a reason to go into another one of their programs when I wasn't even getting recognized for what I was already doing. It's all bullshit? Every class I take, every book I check out to a guy on the block? Why should I bother trying something else when the superintendent is so sure that none of this counts at all?

He couldn't see how I'd changed, and I couldn't see a reason to go to his new program as long as that was true. I had this blindness, right in the middle of all the insight of those days. On the one hand, so much seeing at Old Colony – from walking around the yard with Sean to talking with Dave, preparing the AIDS classes, reading and studying. On the other hand, still, a refusal to look, or a determination to look at one thing but not another.

The fact is I *was* still using drugs. I could prepare for the street in every other way but if I didn't deal with this, too, before getting out, I'd be a fool and I did know that. Hearing men describe how often drugs were what kept them from making it on the outside, it was obvious I had to do something. But I kept putting it off, the way users do.

Drugs were part of life in prison. If you wanted them to be. If you enjoyed the crazy business of chasing deals, making arrangements with someone's friend on the outside or with certain cops who would get you what you wanted if you gave them enough money. When it worked, it almost felt like you'd managed to escape from the prison. You'd pulled something over on them, anyway. And planning all the steps of the process, figuring it out, chasing the guy who'd made a promise or who owed you money – all this was as much of a distraction from prison life as whatever I got from the drugs themselves.

And that wasn't much, these days. If I thought about it, I realized I hadn't really gotten *high* from drugs in years, maybe not even since the time with Seamus in Lewisburg. But like any user, I said I didn't need treatment. I said if they'd just move me to a lower-security prison, everything else would be OK. I was so entrenched in the standoff with the superintendent that I believed if I went into a drug program in his prison I'd be giving in, doing it for him. His hostility was real, but my resistance was real too — and so we stood facing each other, unmoving.

I needed to get out of the stalemate, needed to shake the drug problem loose so that I could look at it head on, apart from the superintendent and whatever he did or didn't believe about me. I needed to be in a new place where I could start fresh and finally deal with this last, crucial thing.

And I got it. I got a fresh start, exactly the one I needed, in my final few months of prison. The superintendent had said *you're gonna wrap up behind the wall*, but then he couldn't stand how nervous I made him, how I seemed to turn up wherever he was. He wouldn't let me forget? OK, I wouldn't let him forget either. He hated the way I seemed to be stalking him, and so after a few weeks he held a classification hearing and I was transferred the next day.

Transferred to Norfolk, the place where I'd started 16 years before. It was sixteen years after Lenny, the wood shop, the home brew. Looking around at Norfolk now, I thought how in those days I couldn't have imagined any of what would follow – not the hell I would go through, not the insight I would eventually find. The truth is, back then I probably couldn't even have imagined *living* sixteen more years in prison.

Norfolk was a medium security prison too, so in that way there was nothing gained by the transfer from Old Colony. It was still "behind the wall." But ripped away from my standoff with the superintendent, I was suddenly able to relax again, to see again. And I saw how much I did want to quit getting high. I saw that it really was the last thing to go, the last thing to deal with. No one was watching to see if I went into a drug program at Norfolk. Certainly no one was trying to make me go. Here, I could just do it quietly. I could just do it for myself.

Norfolk's rehab program had meditation and yard or gym time in the mornings, group meetings in the afternoons and at night, and weekly individual sessions with a counselor. The groups were OK, but it was the talks with the counselor that really did it for me. The counselors were all former users themselves, so they seemed familiar, like a face you recognize in a crowd of strangers. Mine was named Marty, and he'd been clean for about five years. He looked like an old hippie, his hair grey but still long. I came into his office nervous, more interested in asking about the degrees and certificates on the wall than in talking about myself. But then I decided to talk. I decided to tell him everything that had happened at Walpole, everything that the superintendent at Old Colony had been so sure I needed to remember. I figured I'd see what Marty thought.

"You scare me," is what he said. It surprised me, because I knew in some way that's what I'd been trying to do, but I never expected him to come right out and admit I'd succeeded. I'd been trying to come up with stories that made me look like the worst prisoner around. I told him about the riots and the food tray and the beatings before I bothered to tell him about writing stories for Chris or teaching Danny to read or any of the other things that would let him know I wasn't actually so terrible. After all, some people didn't think any of that other stuff mattered. *It's all bullshit.* Was it? What did Marty see when he looked at me?

It was disarming, the way he kept coming out and admitting things. "You make me feel stupid," he said the next time. "Like I can't get through to you." This was a drug program, with counselors who were supposed to know what they were doing. But every time Marty said he didn't know, I trusted him a little more.

It was realer than anything I could remember from the rehab house in North Carolina, where they were always telling me how I felt and where they were so sure they knew exactly how to get in there and break me. I looked at Marty and saw my own doubt looking back at me and I began to realize it was all right. It was all right to wonder sometimes if you were really too fucked up to make it. The wondering was part of caring. It meant you didn't want to fake it this time. It meant you were trying to understand what was real, and to keep it that way.

One day, after I finished telling another story about Walpole, Marty looked at me and said, "I'm glad you're OK." Sitting in that office I realized I was too. Glad, that is. And OK.

Marty knew how to listen. How to just keep quiet and let me roam through all of it — the bad shit that had happened, the fears, the hopes, the struggle to put it all together in a way that made sense. He knew a lot more than it seemed at first, and one of the most important things he knew was how to stay clean. Whenever he did talk about himself, I thought about how his life sounded like one I wouldn't mind living.

"I look at you and I see the chance to be truly free," I admitted after we'd been meeting for several weeks. I hadn't used anything since I'd been in the program. Quietly, without a lot of fanfare, I'd quit not only the drugs but all the work it took to get them in from the street. I was getting out of prison in only a few months, and when I made that comment to Marty he just nodded. He knew I wasn't only talking about him, I was talking about my own freedom. Trying to see it, trying to feel it.

He asked me once if I thought the program at Norfolk was too simple, and I told him simple wasn't so bad. It was working for me. It was simple the way Patricia's crying in our counseling session had been. Or my readiness to quit using. Simple to talk about, maybe, but pretty fucking incredible to feel.

Marty, in fact, wasn't the only one helping me through that time. For the first time in years, I had someone on the outside who cared about me, someone I could write to and dream about. I had Claire.

One thing about chasing drugs from prison is that it hooks you up with people on the street. There was a girl I'd talked to on the phone sometimes from Old Colony, a friend of a guy on my cellblock. One time, she said she had a friend who might like me. Like *what*, I could have wondered, because this girl had never met me. But she knew her friend Claire and I think in some way she was looking out for her. She knew Claire's life had been really rough, and maybe she got the same idea about mine.

I was open enough to the idea of calling. It had been a long time since Anna died, long enough that I thought I could try getting involved with a woman again. I called Claire's number, and right away I liked the sound of her voice. It made me want to listen, it made me want to talk, it made me just let go and be silly, smart, sexy, and cute with her all in the space of a half an hour.

I asked her if she'd write and she said she would. It wasn't long before we were telling each other everything. Whirlwind romance, prison style, where you pour your heart onto the page. Letters you wait for, letters you write and write until you feel like you've crawled inside the letter and you're not in the cell anymore but in that world you've created together, and it doesn't seem unreal even if people try to tell you it is. Some days it seems the realest thing you've got.

Not since Lisa had I let a woman matter that much to me, matter in all the open and hungry places. In that sense, even Anna didn't compare. Visiting me every week for years, Anna had given me so much, but I always knew I was holding something back from her, something essential. Claire only visited me four times, but I let her in. All the way in.

In my letters I told her all about Walpole, the way I'd told Marty. But then I went farther back. I told her about what had happened when I was a kid, how I'd grown up alone, how I always wanted my father back, how I wanted my mother back, too, even though she was there in the house, how I ended up in prison. Claire told me that she'd been raped too, when she was young, and that later on her husband had abused their kids and he was gone now but she'd learned not to trust anybody. There was so much hurt in the world, but when Claire and I wrote to each other, I started to think maybe we could stand together against it. Maybe we could finally get free.

On one of her visits she brought her kids with her, young kids who didn't hide how curious they were about this place I was in. "Are you a bad guy?" one of them asked, and I laughed and grabbed him and pretended I was going to bite, and somehow he got it, he knew he didn't need to be scared of me, and after that the four kids started climbing all over me and making me laugh. Something opened up inside me on that visit, enough so I could see what I'd missed all the years when other men were getting married and having children. I wondered if it was too late. I looked over at Claire who was watching her kids climb on me. It was only a few more months until I'd be getting out.

And then the bomb fell. I'd been in love with Claire for about a year and a half when she wrote to tell me she'd slept with someone else. As soon as I felt the blow I realized it was one I *remembered* feeling – this is what happens, this shot through the heart. She slept with another guy because she had to, thought she had to, because love in letters and hopes and plans wasn't enough for her. I hated sex because it caused all the trouble I'd ever had – sex people couldn't keep from wanting, sex people couldn't keep from having, sex that made people hurt each other and hurt themselves. Why couldn't Claire have waited just a couple more months for me to get out? Why was she that weak, why did she need the kind of proof I couldn't give from a prison cell but was *going* to give her as soon as I could, oh shit I was going to.

"You were in love with a piece of paper," Eddie, my Norfolk cellmate, told me. "There'll be plenty of other women when you get out. Why are you so hung up on this one?"

Because there *was* a lot of love and hope and planning in those letters. Because when you open up to someone and tell your secrets, you know they're walking around with that part of you inside them, always, no matter what else happens. And because I was getting out of prison soon and thought I was going to go live with Claire. I thought she would be how I started my new life.

It took me a long time, a lot of devastated days of talking about it, to figure out what the problem really was for Claire. I'd been so sure I wasn't enough for her, that she left me for the one thing I couldn't give. But the problem wasn't *not enough*. The problem for Claire was *too much*. She always told me I was too good for her, that what we had was more than she deserved.

Not everybody *wants* to drink life straight up. I couldn't understand why Claire would wreck what we were planning until I figured out that maybe the plans were exactly what scared her. It scared her to think of me getting out, ready for everything. She needed to wreck it not because it was bad, but because it was good – and because it was getting so close to real.

Every day after Claire's letter I came into Marty's office looking like someone had just run over my dog. "How am I gonna get through *this* one, Marty?" I asked. But he told me I would, and the surprising thing is that I truly did. I felt my way through it. Hurting, doubting, stunned at the way I got the rug pulled out from under me again. But I was taking it – that was the difference. I wasn't numb this time. I could feel myself feeling it. I didn't have to get rid of her or find a way to tear my own aching heart out of my chest.

When I stole my mother's car at 14 and ended up in the county jail, I told the cops I was 18. A phone call to my mother got them the truth, and right away they were at my cell door: "Harrison, come out here." They sounded so urgent, I thought I was in trouble for something else.

"Are you OK?" one cop asked as he explained that they were transferring me to a juvenile facility. "Did anyone hurt you?"

What a long time coming that question was. And now that someone thought to ask, I had nothing to say. No one had hurt me there in the jail. I took the question the way they meant it and told them I was fine. I was too tightly coiled by then to let the other answer spill out: *actually, I'm not OK, and someone did hurt me once, and I thought you'd never ask.* When you want something long enough and it doesn't come, you close yourself up against it and even when it does finally come, receiving it isn't so easy. There was real concern in the cop's question, but all I could absorb was the information: this is the kind of thing that happens in jail. And just because it didn't happen this time doesn't mean it won't.

Everyone wonders about it. When I talk to people about prison now, I see them working up to the question: is it true ...?

Well, I wondered too. In the van on the way to Walpole that very first day, one of the clearest thoughts in my head was *where can I get a knife?* It was the question then, as it had been for so long: how can I protect myself? I looked at the men sitting chained to me and I made a decision: I will not let it happen again. Will not surrender that way, even if it turns out that's what it takes to survive here. No, I'll kill him or myself first.

Soon enough, I learned that any spare piece of steel could be made into a knife. That part was simple. But with or without steel of my own, I never even came close to being raped in prison. The rules turned out to be both simpler and more complicated than I expected.

"See that guy? He's a chickenhawk," someone said, pointing to a guy across the yard. I'd only been in prison a couple of days and I didn't know what he meant, but it was easy enough to guess. I thought of birds and men who prey on the weak. I thought of the chickens on my grandfather's farm, the hands around my neck and the warning. I understood about chickenhawks, and mentally I was already gripping the knife: *never again, never again.*

But here was the first thing that was different: in prison, I wasn't the kind of kid a chickenhawk would pick. Even though I didn't go for young boys, I understood how to search out weakness and hunt it down. I was more predator than prey, and that was what they saw. And I wasn't doing some easy sentence for a nothing crime. I was doing 28-30 years for armed robbery and it was clear I wasn't someone to mess with. So no one even tried. Even when an obvious kid-chaser like Robbie checked me out the way he checked everyone out, he didn't bother me once I let him know I wasn't interested. It was easier to say no than I ever imagined. It turned out I'd arrived with all the protection I needed.

The chickenhawks weren't going to be a threat to me. It took only a couple of months to figure that out. It took longer to realize that without that threat, I had room for some real questions. Years after the rapist had done his damage, after the hustling with Kenny and Lane, after the blurred confusion of the year with Tom, after my own crime against gay men had landed me in prison, I was on my way to seeing some things I'd never seen before.

What does it mean when men get together? Always a hustle and a lie, always a mask for their own selfish desire. That was the knowledge I carried with me in the van on the way to Walpole, and I hung onto it. But now what about Sean, what about Seamus, what about Chris or Bobby? These were men who mattered to me now and the mattering was good. Good enough to pry my tightly held cynicism loose.

And then there was Jacko. Jacko, the tough queen who accepted himself so fully you couldn't help accepting him. Jacko, who showed me that things could be a little more complicated than I was used to letting them be.

The rumor had swept through 10 Block: "Jacko and his kid are coming down." His kid? A man in his forties with a "kid" for sex? I was ready to hate him. And then they put him on my tier and he surprised me — a real, no-bullshit guy, someone I'd have liked if I didn't know any better. I asked him what he'd done to end up in 10 Block and he said he'd stabbed a guy who called his kid a name. And the other guy was a lot bigger than he was.

I tried to put the pieces together. Jacko looked out for this guy Derek. He stood up for him, stood up for himself. I always thought guys like Jacko would do anything to get what they wanted and then run the minute loyalty and honor were on the line. But Jacko didn't run. So — cautiously — I didn't either. I hung around enough to see what this guy was all about.

It turned out Jacko wasn't only tougher than I expected. He had an even bigger surprise. I saw it when we were back at Walpole together after I returned from Lewisburg. By this time I liked to hang out in his cell while he cooked linguine in his hot pot. We talked about things in an easy way – cards, because Jacko loved to play, or our mothers, because Jacko's had died when he was young. I told him my mother was there when I was growing up but she wasn't *really* there. It was out of my mouth before I realized what it meant: I was letting Jacko matter to me too. Sitting around waiting for the linguine to cook, I was telling him things.

Derek was there too. While Jacko listened to me he was rubbing Derek's feet, caressing him with a gentle hand, and even as I kept talking a part of me was going *holy shit, look at that.* Wasn't he embarrassed? Didn't he know what shame was? But the thing is, what he was doing wasn't even shameful. It was kind. It was actually tender. That was what they had, and they let me see it. Two men who were giving something to each other instead of taking, and Jacko so comfortable in his own skin, so ready to let others figure out how to deal with who he was.

So I began to figure it out. I put it together with every other new thought blossoming inside my head and I asked myself, *what's the harm here?*

None that I could see, but I had to be sure. I got Derek alone and asked him if he really liked what he had going with Jacko.

"Yeah," he said, looking at me straight on. "Me and Jacko are cool. He's not making me do anything I don't want to do."

Right. That was the point. I saw it as clearly as I'd ever seen anything. So when Jacko asked me the next day if I'd mind being their lookout, I took one look at his mischievous grin and said sure. He and Derek hung a sheet over the cell door and I stood at the end of the tier looking out for cops. They had their privacy and even though I got a little jealous sometimes, thinking about how they had each other to turn to while I had only pictures in magazines, I couldn't help smiling at how far I'd come. Jacko liked men, I liked women. That was just how it was. And I was standing here protecting someone I would once have despised. Protecting him because I *could.* Because I didn't need to destroy him anymore.

Tenderness may be prison's greatest secret – more hidden even than the brutality. And sometimes even more frightening. The soft center, the quiet openness of Jacko's hand on Derek's foot, or my confession to

Sean, or Danny's to me. What an unexpected reprieve it was, each time. It meant the sentence of isolation and shame that the rapist had handed down to me all those years ago didn't have to be a life sentence. Under that burning sun there might actually be some shade. Some place that has not been scarred; some part of me that can still be touched without harm.

I protected Jacko and Derek because I could, and later I protected a kid named Mark because I had to. I met Mark at Norfolk. He had just arrived in prison, and I was very close to wrapping up my sentence and getting out. He only had three years to do but you could tell he was scared. I worried about him. He wasn't stupid, but he was only 17.

"Do you have to be violent to make it in here?" he asked me one day. I didn't answer him right away. I was thinking about how complicated the question was, in prison and on the street too. Do you *have* to be violent? I wanted to tell him what Bobby had taught me, how you don't have to go looking for ways to be tough, how you can learn to stand your ground without deliberately searching for ways to prove yourself. Mark had fought a guy who insulted his girlfriend. He got charged with assault and battery and ended up here. I turned his question around and asked him,

"Did you feel like you had to do it? Or did you ever feel like you could just walk away from it?"

In other words, what was it actually like that day? What went on inside your head, inside your body, how did you feel to do it, what happened what happened what *actually* happened? The questions it's so hard for a courtroom to ask. I could picture Mark in court, trying for all the toughness his scrawny body could project. But now all that was over and done and he was sitting in a cell trying to answer my questions. By the time he got to the part about his mother and how she hated seeing him in prison, he broke down and cried. I watched him, thinking about how young he was.

"With me that's OK," I said after the tears had stopped. "But be careful. I wouldn't open up like that in front of everyone around here."

I was trying to teach him to look for real friends, but look carefully. As I watched him break open and let those tears spill out, I realized there was something decent and unspoiled inside this kid, something no one had gotten to yet. Something I would try as hard as I could to keep safe.

One of the chickenhawks has his eye on Mark. Never again, never again. There are just some things I will not stand for. There's this boy here and OK he's no saint

but he's no monster either, I mean he really could go either way and you just want to take him and make him what you are. You want him for yourself and all I can say is, not if I have anything to do with it. 'Cause I've watched this long enough and I'm tired of it. This is a kid and he's scared and he's fuckin' right to be scared and you're not going to move in on him and destroy him. Yeah, you're just trying to survive here, and Christ only knows what's already been done to you, but there's just got to be some stopping it some time. There's got to be some kid who gets free.

I got a couple of other guys to go with me, to tell this chickenhawk to back off of Mark. I had to talk to these other guys first, let them get to know Mark and see him the way I did. It didn't take long, even for someone like Chuck who liked young guys himself and joked, "But Reb, *I* wanted Mark." Even he was just kidding around, because he saw Mark was a good kid and he didn't truly want to mess with that any more than I did. So with three guys flanking me, I went to see this chickenhawk and I told it to him in a way he could hear.

"Listen, Mark's a good kid from a good family. He's doing a short sentence and we really don't want to fuck that up. Don't you agree?"

He agreed. He had to. But I'd given him a way to do it. I let him look like he was backing off because he decided to, not because Rebel threatened him. Even if he understood perfectly, even if he knew without a doubt that I'd be coming back if he didn't get my meaning the first time. I let him have his pride, and we didn't have any trouble.

So I'd done what I could to keep Mark safe. *I won't let him take anything from you* I was saying to Mark, same as I'd said it to Tom all those years ago when the man wouldn't pay up what he owed. Each time, I was really saying it about myself: I will not let anything else be taken. The difference is, this time around I knew what I really meant, and knew how to do it without the gun. So many years later, I finally understood that I wasn't powerless anymore. I could gather up everything I had inside me, and with only that determination as my weapon, I could look someone right in the face and say *don't hurt this boy.*

"So you're going home soon," the cop said as he passed my cell, and there was no mocking in it, just interest. *Home.* I thought about telling him how scared I was, how the truth was I didn't have any idea *where* I was going. If going home meant going back where you came from, I'd be heading to North Carolina, but I'd known for a long time that that was a bad idea. It was going to be hard enough to start over. I didn't need old connections, old roads that didn't lead anywhere I wanted to go.

For months I'd thought home was going to be Claire's, but now that that was over, what could I do? I didn't know Boston at all. I'd come up from Florida to do the crime, fled to New Jersey, and then when the cops brought me back, all I ever saw of Boston was a jail cell. And then a lot of different prison cells around the state. I wasn't sure I *could* make Boston my home, even if I wanted to.

In another three months Norfolk was going to open its doors and let me out, and where was I going to sleep that night? Maybe there's a reason prisoners talk about getting released "to the street." I knew I was going to have to do something about this while I still had time, or I *would* end up on the street that first night out. I was miserable about Claire, but I wasn't knocked all the way down. I told myself it would be stupid to give up before I even got out there.

I wrote to some shelters and halfway houses I heard about. One wrote back. It was a place in the city for homeless ex-offenders, and they said I could come there if I wanted to. So all right. That was a bed for the first few nights. But every time I pictured it, the idea of sleeping in a shelter seemed so lonely and impersonal that I kept thinking there had to be another way. What I really wanted was to be around real people, people who were used to doing things in the world, instead of a bunch of guys fresh out of prison, as scared and new as I figured I was going to be.

I said to myself that there had to be organizations that cared about prisoners, and then I remembered Joan, whom I'd met at Old Colony a few times. She worked for a prisoners' advocacy organization, one that a lot of guys wrote to when they had a problem. Whenever I ran into her we'd joke back and forth a little, enjoying the conversation. I didn't know her, really, but it seemed like anyone who came into prisons when they didn't have to would be willing to give someone like me the benefit of the doubt. I figured I could at least write to her and see what happened.

I wrote telling her I had no place to stay when I got out except a shelter, and I wondered if there was any chance I could stay at her house. She wrote back and asked how long I was talking about, and I said not long, just time enough to get on my feet, find some work if I could. And she agreed. She took a chance and said OK. She even said she would come and get me when I got released, or if she couldn't make it, she would be sure someone was there to do it.

So now I knew where I was going, and the countdown really began. When you're deep in the middle of a sentence as long as mine, the release date is nothing more than a notation in the files. It's so far off you can't imagine it, and it hardly matters if it's listed as one day or another. But this close to freedom, the exact day was all I could think about. As often as they let me, I checked with the records office at Norfolk to see what they thought my date was.

I knew it could change any time. I'd seen it happen: a guy is counting down to a certain day and then suddenly the records office discovers 100 days of good time they say he lost somewhere along the line, and there he is, waiting 100 more days. I'd lost so much good time during the years in segregation, and then I'd earned a lot of it back later on, but you could drive yourself crazy adding and subtracting, checking your own calculations against what they said in the records office. And even as the day got closer, I couldn't trust it. I figured I could easily be getting ready, only to wake up and hear *sorry, you've got another month to do.* After seventeen years full of surprise moves, anything seemed possible. Still, the closer I got, the more I fixed on the June day they had listed for me, and acted as if that day would truly be the day I got out.

One week left, and I'm hardly sleeping. I'm hoarding hope and worry but I'm giving away as much as I can from my cell. I give my dictionaries to a couple of guys who I know will use them. I give postcards — everyone here loves pictures of the outside. I give a couple of pairs of sweatpants and shorts, just hanging on to a couple for myself so I'll have something to start out with. And I keep the books that have meant so much to me.

By the final night, the cell is almost bare. What I've got fits into a small carton. What I've got that people can see, anyway.

Wake up and it comes. The day. This is the one prison routine I don't know the procedure for. What do I have to go through before I can leave? It turns out they have to get someone to walk me over to the Administration Gate so I can sign the release papers, and the call doesn't come, doesn't come, I'm sitting and waiting. Finally the cop comes and I start walking with him across the yard, and some guys are following along, walking with me as far as they can go, and they're chattering at me but I can't take it in, I've got nothing but life and freedom on my mind.

I'm handed the papers that say my sentence is done, served in full. I sign them and look up expectantly at the cops. I'm free now, they've agreed to it, so what happens next?

What happens is they lock me in a cell right there in the administration area. I start yelling at the one cop who's standing there, trying to make him tell me what's going on, why they're still keeping me here. "I'm a repatriated citizen," I tell him, and for a minute I just stop and think about how I love the sound of those words. "And it's time for me to go home."

"Shut the fuck up, Harrison," is what he says. "Shut up or you'll be here until midnight. I can do that, you know. I can do that if you don't shut up."

He can make me wait just because he feels like it. They're going to take every last bit of me that they can. This is every prison moment of crazy frustration, not knowing what to expect, and he is every cop who tried to make me beg for mercy, who wanted to use every last ounce of power. I mumble *what an asshole* and sit back down, and an hour goes by before I ask again what the problem is. He ignores me. Is my freedom meaningless? And will Joan's daughter, who I know is waiting out there for me, give up and go home?

At two hours I ask again, and he finally tells me that they need to get someone who can walk me out, through the front trap where visitors enter and prisoners – sometimes – leave. It's not more than 100 yards from here to the trap and after waiting for two hours in this cell I just lose it, I yell at him that it's been 17 years and now I've got to wait two more hours even though I've signed the papers and I'm legally free? Is it that hard to find someone who can walk me out?

Another 30 minutes pass, for good measure, and then the other cop finally comes, and I see it's one I know. He smiles and says, "Reb, how are you?" but all I can say is "I'll be fine if I can just get the fuck out of here." He hands me something and at first I can't even see what it is, but then I understand: it's my wallet. From 17 years ago. The wallet I had on me when I was arrested, taken away from me, along with my belt, at the first strip search. It's followed me from institution to institution but it was never OK for me to have it until this moment, and it's like being given an artifact from a grave. I just stare at it, thinking who was the man who held this wallet, do I even remember shoving it into the pocket of my pants, do I remember the day I had to surrender it to them? It makes me dizzy, for a minute, but then I look up and see that it really is time to go.

The cop walks me the hundred yards and then out through the trap and there in the waiting room I see Miranda, Joan's daughter, and I'm so grateful she didn't leave. She comes to hug me and says *it's OK* and all at once it does start to be.

The cop is standing there watching us and then he says he'll carry my box of property out to the car. I tell him I'll do it but he says no, I'm honored to carry your stuff after all you've been through. I can't believe I've heard him right. He carries it, we put it in the trunk, and then he holds his hand out to shake mine. It's like the warden at Gardner all over again, the surprise of it, and this cop *doesn't* say to me what the cop said to Sean when he walked him out, instead he wishes me good luck, and it makes me wonder if the world is really going to be this way, open and welcoming, if maybe it really will take me back.

How could it happen, that all the paradoxes of prison were packed inside those final hours: the cop who swore he could keep me there all day and the one who said he was honored to help me out? I'm standing in the parking lot, halfway between that life and this new one, thinking that somehow the world is both, brutal and tender, and so what we have to do is decide – decide what we want to become, and decide what to remember, what to hold on to.

I get in the car with Miranda, still reeling from all of this, telling her how angry I was at the waiting and how scared that she'd leave and how grateful I am that she's here now, driving me away. "Do you want anything?" she asks, and I say the first thing I think of: bubble gum. And a soda. She pulls over at a convenience store and we go in, and the shelves overwhelm me because there are a hundred kinds of bubble gum and I have to choose, I *get* to choose, and I can't even really take in the fact that I'm standing here in this store. And then I go to open the cooler to get a soda, but I don't know how to open it, I can't see exactly how to do it. I'm sure the guy at the counter is looking at me. Everyone must see that I've just arrived, that I have no idea what I'm doing. Is it always going to feel like this?

Back in the car, looking out the window as we drive, it's like that trip from 10 Block to Gardner, only I'm not handcuffed to anybody, there's no one guarding me, and I have as much right to this road, these trees, as anybody in any car. And it's Miranda driving the car, not a cop, and she's already asked me what I want, and I know she would stop again if I said I wanted something else. *Thank you*, I keep telling her, thank you and your mother, it's so incredible that you're doing this for me.

We get to the apartment and I'm amazed by all the color, all the things on the walls and the shelves. Miranda stands watching me as I look at everything, and then she shows me to my room and I collapse on the bed. All I can think is how soft it is, how much softer than a prison bed. I lie there for a minute thinking *this is where I will sleep tonight. This is a place where people live.* It's going to be a while before I really feel the impact of this day, a day that has taken me from a prison cell into a room in a house, but I know this: being let out is one thing. Being let in is something else again, and breathtaking.

They call it the re-entry process. As a released prisoner, you're coming back to a world you left long ago. But the world is so different, and you're so different, that half the time it feels more like trying to enter a place you've never been before and aren't sure you have any right to be. And might not know *how* to live in even if they let you.

I was up against the odds, trying to outrun the high-risk period when many ex-cons get so overwhelmed by that feeling of being an alien that they get themselves sent back to prison, where at least they don't have to figure out how to create their lives every morning. But the rebel in me *liked* the challenge of those odds, even as they scared the shit out of me. I wanted to be one of the ones who made it.

After getting my ID, I knew the next thing I had to do was find a job. A friend of Miranda's did steam cleaning for businesses – huge dirty jobs that he let me help out with for a while. So that was something right away, before I even had a chance to panic about who would hire me or how I was going to explain what I'd been doing for the past 17 years.

Then a friend of Joan's found another way for me to help out. She gave me some work around her house – landscaping, painting, fixing the roof. "How'd you learn to do that?" she asked, surprised, the first time I finished a job. "From *This Old House*," I told her, laughing. Hours of watching TV in prison, watching other people do things instead of getting to do them myself, and now it turned out TV wasn't just a way to pass the time – it was a form of job training, too.

So many people were taking chances on me, giving me a way to get started. It was more than I'd imagined possible, and more than a lot of guys got. After a few weeks, I began to think about getting steady work, and the amazing thing was that I ended up with a choice. At a conference with Joan, I met a union lawyer who used to work at a state school for people with severe mental retardation. We got to talking, and he said if I wanted to interview at that school, he would put in a good word for me. So when I went in for the interview, I was up front about my prison background, and it was OK – I got offered a job as an orderly on the psychiatric ward.

I was about to take it when I ran into an old friend from prison. He said he had a job at a school in Charlestown and he thought I could probably work there too. He said it was a good place. I talked to the boss and

I liked the feel of the school, so when she said I could work part-time as a janitor, I decided to take it.

It was a school for kids no other school wanted. They had emotional problems, learning problems, behavior problems, or all three. Whether the causes were childhood brain damage or childhood abuses, the kids ended up having a really hard time.

For the first few months, I just concentrated on trying to be the best janitor they'd ever seen. But while I was washing the floor or cleaning the toilets, I paid attention to what was going on around me. I'd see a kid cursing at a teacher and then slamming out of the room, and I'd put down my mop and go after him, following his cloud of rage. I'd sit with him and let him know I was listening.

After a while it got so I was doing as much listening and talking as cleaning, and so they promoted me to Behavior Manager. That meant I *had* to intervene whenever a kid flew off the handle. I had to try to help the kids control themselves, but I also had to try to help the kids and teachers understand what made control so hard to hold onto in the first place.

In some ways it was probably the hardest job I could've stumbled into. But after a few months of doing it, I didn't want to do anything else.

"Fuck you! I hate you!" the kid is yelling. I've been called every name these kids can think of, and some days it's hard to believe we're getting anywhere. This boy has just picked up a chair and hurled it across the room, and I tell him what that means, that he'll have to leave school for the rest of the day. But later I do some asking around and I find out he's worried because his brother's in jail and his mother is sick. I pull the kid aside the next day and we talk for a while about what's going on and how rough things are for him. How can you manage behavior if you don't understand what's really causing it? I *know* these kids. I know what's under all that anger, what's packed inside all the four-letter words. Fear, longing, despair. They don't even realize how well I know.

Sometimes I end up doing things that a teacher would do, like sitting with a girl and helping her with her algebra assignment. She's struggling with it and I show her another way to do it and suddenly she bursts out, "I love you! You always straighten out my thinking, whenever I think I can't do something." The surprise of her gratitude spreads inside me, warm and sustaining. And then she comes back the next day and fights with a friend instead of doing algebra, and the boy who threw the chair is in trouble again, and I start to wonder if they're ever going to learn.

But what did I expect? Isn't this exactly how it goes? Change doesn't come just because I wish it for them, but I have to stick around and keep wishing anyway, because if I can stay with them even when they try to shake me off, I'm doing more than most of them imagined anyone would do. They are Danny, Sean, Mark – they are every closed up and hurting kid I ever wanted to reach and wanted to believe could change. And so that means they are me, too.

The kids respect me when they hear I've done prison time, but I know the respect only means something if I can use it to turn them in another direction. One day two kids ask me to hook them up with something, to help them get a gun and figure out what they can do with it, and I shake my head no. "Listen," I say. "You really don't want to do that. I've been there, and look at me – I've got a life full of regret. Look at all the years I wasted over violence."

I get a picture of Walpole and hang it on the wall in my office.
"Is that where you were?" a kid asks one day when he comes in.
"Yes," I answer, and I make sure he knows the picture's not up there because I'm proud of it. It's up as a reminder to me – and to them – of where I never want to be again.

It was wonderful not having to keep prison a secret. My boss knew where I'd been and she trusted me anyway. The day she let me sign checks from the school's bank account was the day I was convinced people didn't see me as a thief anymore. And she let me leave work to go to college classes and make up the hours later – another sign of how strongly she believed in me.

The ones who have college degrees hardly ever come back to prison. That's what we always heard, and every statistic confirmed it. I'd hung onto that hope all those years of taking classes at Walpole and Old Colony. And then when I was finally close to getting my degree *and* close to getting out of prison, the rumors started flying. "If that federal crime bill passes," I heard one of the school staff mutter, "they're going to cut the Pell Grants for prisoners." We saw it in the newspapers too. All the indignant quotes from people who said 43 million dollars shouldn't be going to murderers and thieves while good kids couldn't afford an education.

The Crime Bill passed, the Pell Grants did get cut, and it turned out that the prisoners' allotment was a separate budget anyway. Taking $43 million away from us didn't directly give any more money to those good kids. It just meant that young guys coming in to prison now weren't going to hear men like Chris talk about short stories or men like Allan Hunter talk about Shakespeare. And it meant that with only a couple of credits left to go, I had no way of finishing my degree.

It was like the Old Colony superintendent all over again. So close, and suddenly the message was, "Tough shit, we're not letting you go any further." Climb and climb up that rope that tethers you to the possibility of another life, and then the rope snaps and you lie there angry and hurting on the prison floor.

But my friend Eddie calmed me down again, just the way he'd calmed me down after Claire. "If you're that close," he said, "you can finish up when you get out." He said I would probably still be able to get financial aid. "So you won't come out with your degree in your hand like you wanted to, but you'll get it," Eddie said, and he was right.

I took classes at the University of Massachusetts the fall after I got out. I sat in classrooms on a real campus, surrounded by all kinds of students, including one I'd never have sat in class with in the old days.

It was the first day of Social Theory. We were introducing ourselves, saying what we did for a living. I said I worked at a school, and then the man next to me said he was a corrections officer.

I couldn't believe it. For the next two weeks I watched him, and what I saw was a smart guy who really cared about earning the grades. He didn't need the degree for his job – you can be a CO with only a high school diploma. He was obviously interested in what he was doing. The third week, I said, "You remember I told you I worked at a school? Well, I do – but I also just did 17 years in prison."

Now it was his turn to watch me, but soon enough we were talking. He told me he wanted to work at Walpole because he wanted to see what it was like at the maximum security prison, and I tried to talk him out of it. I said, "I'll *tell* you what it's like," and I let him know some of the worst things that had happened there. I even brought him some literature from the prisoners' advocacy organization. He read it, he listened to me, but he still kept saying he wanted to try working there. "Look," he explained. "I'm going to go there and try to be fair." In the end I respected his attitude. And I liked the way it felt to talk to a cop on the outside, as two students in a class, two men trying to think about what we were doing.

Almost exactly a year after my release, I got to put on a cap and gown and graduate with hundreds of other students. I graduated *summa cum laude* with a degree in Sociology, and I stood up there thinking about the day I'd taken the GED fourteen years earlier. "See?" Bobby had said back then, after I told him my score, and now I could picture his smiling face in my mind. I wanted to say it back to him: See! See where I am, see how all this has turned out.

Graduation morning, I'd been heading across the parking lot when a reporter stopped me and said she was doing a story on adult graduates. Did I mind answering a few questions?

"You got lucky," I told her, and I couldn't help grinning. "I've got a great story for you."

I was used to talking to reporters by then. Going with Joan to all kinds of speaking events had given me the chance to be a prison activist along with her, so I got to talk about what went on in prison, what helped me, what didn't. In some way it felt like I owed that public speaking to everyone. I owed it to the people I had hurt so many years ago. I owed it to *anyone* who'd been hurt by someone like me. And I owed it to those who were still locked up in prison.

Back when I'd been in prison only a few months, I had made friends with a guy who was about to be released. I gave him some money just before he left, to help him get on his feet. He got out, and I never heard from him again. After that, I figured that making friends with guys who were serving short sentences was a set-up for more betrayal. They left and never looked back. You'd have better luck getting a citizen on the street to write to you than these guys, most of the time.

I didn't understand it until I was out myself, riding the bus to work, holding an envelope addressed to a lifer. Tears were rolling down my cheeks. How could I account for my own freedom when his was impossible? How could I even think about prison while trying to make my way through the days of this new life? It was hard to remember it, hard to forget it, hard to know where to put it in my mind.

When we were in 10 Block feeling like we'd been thrown away behind a wall so thick no one else could see what was happening to us, we were mostly right. Most people on the outside don't think much about prisoners or care much about what goes on. The ex-cons know, but they know too well. Once you get out, keeping in touch is harder and more painful than you ever imagine it will be. And so is trying to explain prison to anyone else. But whenever I thought it would be easier to just keep quiet, stop reliving and retelling everything, the thought of my friends inside would keep me talking.

Anna had visited me every week in 10 Block no matter how crazy I looked, no matter how much I rocked back and forth and ranted about whatever outrageous thing had happened that day. She would tell me to put my hand up to the grate and she would hold my finger – the only part she could reach – until I calmed down.

Hard as it is, I keep talking because I hope that my words might be for other prisoners what Anna's hand was for me: the link that reminds them they are not forgotten.

In addition to the long prison sentence, the judge in 1978 had given me three years' probation, which would start the day I got out. "Maybe somewhere down the line something will change you," he'd said, but it was obvious he wasn't laying any money on that idea. It might happen, it might not. When I got out, he wanted to be sure there was protection at the other end, too – some way to keep watch and see whether it really was safe to let me re-enter this world.

The probation officer came down hard on me the first time we met. "You will be in my office whenever I tell you to be here," he said, stern as any cop. "You miss a day, and I'll put you back inside. You get a new arrest, I'll put you inside. Put prison behind you, rebuild your life, and we won't have any problems."

Rebuild your life. Did he understand how much I wanted that? At first he said I had to come in every two weeks. After three months, he said I only had to come in once a month. I could see it in his eyes when I told him about my job and the college classes and the public speaking: he believed I was doing OK. I was making it through the high-risk time.

"You know, a lot of people expect guys like you to fail," he told me.

"I know."

"I saw your name in the paper the other day," he said, looking at me thoughtfully. He'd seen me quoted in an article about prison issues. "I'm really glad you're doing something positive about everything you've seen. I'm really glad someone like you is speaking out."

I left his office that day thinking about how differently people saw me now. At college, at work, even in the probation office, people kept showing me that I had a right to everything this new life was giving me. I knew there were plenty of people out here who saw it the other way, too – people who believed I'd already gotten more than I deserved. And the truth was, there was something inside *me* that felt the same way.

Some days in 10 Block, it was possible to sit in the cell, so absorbed in the book I was reading or the letter I was writing that it felt as if the walls were gone. As if I was somehow free no matter what else was true.

In the worst days of segregation, I had learned to make some kind of freedom inside me, a space no one could violate or claim.

10 Block is all about paradox, but freedom has paradox in it too, and it took me a while to realize it. It has to do with the ways we cage ourselves. Sometimes during that first year of being out, consumed with some small frustration, I would pace back and forth until I suddenly realized what I was doing: I was pacing the exact length of a prison cell. The imprisonment was part of me. Even here, even now.

And so there were bad days too. Days when the smallest insult or irritation sent me into a rage, days when anyone in authority seemed like a prison cop and I'd be back there in my head, feeling the way I'd felt then. And I hated feeling it. I wanted so badly to believe I'd won, prison hadn't broken me. It was hard to admit that some parts of me *were* broken, or at least imperfectly healed.

In prison, you know who the enemy is. You hate *the man*, you hate the place you're locked in, and any time you're angry you can focus it there. But outside, especially when everything is going well, you have to realize that the enemy is also somehow inside you. If you're feeling locked up and miserable and alone, it isn't only prison that's doing it. There are internal walls, internal demons to wrestle with, and those enemies can be harder to fight.

Some days I looked around at all the good things in my life and I still felt I couldn't do it, couldn't come back all the way, couldn't be a man among men when I'd missed so many pieces along the way. Some days I was scared in ways I didn't even know how to explain. I'd walk down the street with all the people around me and feel as different from them, as exiled and apart, as I'd felt during the darkest prison days. Or as I'd felt on the long-ago night when I stood inside my uncle's beer joint, looking around me and thinking *no one knows*.

I didn't want to feel like this anymore. I wanted to just be grateful, I wanted to just be free. But when I couldn't *feel* the gratitude or the freedom, I would give in and have a beer. It softened that harsh edge between me and everyone else, on days when I felt nothing else could. But beer was as slick and cunning now as it had ever been. It promised comfort and then turned on you afterwards, leaving you worse off than you were before. It took me a long time to understand that beer could never be the answer to exile. It could never really bring me back.

On that exhilarating car ride with Miranda my first day out of prison, I had no idea how hard freedom would sometimes feel. How much learning there still was to do.

Since I've been out of prison, I've ridden the subway to the end of the line and driven the winding side streets of my new city. But this road to Winston-Salem was the one road I didn't want to be on. I'm coming home to see the passage of years in the new six-lane highway, in the downtown stores I don't recognize. I'm coming home to see who I am in my mother's eyes. I'm coming home to watch my mother die.

So much time has passed, and I still don't know how to be her son, either up close or at a distance.

The day I got out of prison, I'd called her from Joan's apartment.

"I'm out," I told her. She'd waited 17 years to hear that, but she'd been waiting even longer to hear that I was coming home and that wasn't what I was saying now.

"I don't know why you don't come home. You have a perfectly good bed here," she complained, and the familiar mix of loyalty and anger, guilt and fear, began to kick around inside of me. I forced myself to see my college degree, so close I could almost touch it, and I told her I needed to stay in Boston to graduate. I had a good place to stay, and I'd find a job and come visit when I could. I fought the impulse to give in; I ignored the voice in my head saying *you've hurt her enough; can't you do what she's asking now?*

"If you ever need to come home, you can," she tried once more, and I didn't hear it as the reasonable offer of a safety net that it probably was. I was sure she was doubting I could make it on my own. I hung up without telling her how much of me feared she was right.

Now it's just about a year since that conversation. All these months in Boston, I thought I was preparing for this trip, thought I would only come back to North Carolina when I had enough to show for myself. But it turns out it doesn't matter whether I'm ready. My mother is dying of liver cancer and there's no pretending I'll get another chance. When Grady called and told me she was sick, I didn't even ask what was wrong. Didn't dare to find out. Joan took charge, called the doctor and made him stop hedging and equivocating by asking him, "If it were your mother, what would you do?" "I'd come home," he admitted, and that was enough for Joan. "If you don't go now, you'll regret it forever," she told me. So here we are, driving, not knowing what it will be like when we get there.

"Am I going to die?" my mother asks me, looking up from the hospital bed we've set up in my brother's old room.

When was the last time I told my mother the truth? How long since truth didn't feel like something she'd use against me later on? I look at her and remember every impossible conversation, everything we've never managed to tell each other. I'm seven years old and burning my toys, everything acrid and melting and ruined, and she screams at me, "What do you think you're doing? You're going to end up in prison some day!" I stare at the molten plastic and I don't have the words to say *I'm your son. If you're hurting, I am too.* I'm 21, calling her from the Charles Street Jail and calling only because the cop says "Call your mother" in a way I can't refuse. I tell her I've been arrested for armed robbery and attempted murder, and she cries, "That can't be right, you wouldn't do that." "You don't know me very well," I answer. She hasn't known me in years. Everything I've tried to tell her has gotten garbled on the way until I've given up trying. "I guess I won't be coming home for a while" is all I manage to add, and she hangs up. She can't say *I'm your mother. If you're in trouble, I am too.*

And now I've come home, and she's asking me to tell her the truth about the end of her own life.

"Yeah, you are, Mom."

"Well, I thought *something*," she says, and I have to laugh. Something indeed. Something to bring both your sons here together, not to mention a lawyer and a preacher too.

"*When* am I going to die?" she asks later on. Having gotten one straight answer, she's going to try for another, as if it's possible for us to look up the exact time and warn her of it. We do what we can. We sit by her bed; we fill the rooms of the house.

"Lord have mercy, my hands look terrible," she exclaims one day, so I take her hands in mine and do her nails for her. I know how she wants to look; I know at least this much about what matters to her. After I'm done, I hold on to her hands for another minute, but she pulls away, saying, "You're the *touchingest* kid I've ever seen." I admit it: I wanted to touch her. I wanted to feel her touching me.

That evening, I stand in the doorway and see Grady climb into the bed with her, sobbing the way grown men sob, as if something is being ripped out of him.

"I'm going to do everything in my power to be with you," he swears, committing himself to her again, promising to live a life that will get him into heaven. She strokes his hair and tries to comfort him. I've never seen Grady cry and I've hardly ever seen them touch each other. I stand caught in the doorway, not moving in or out of the room. I worry that I'm intruding, but I can't turn away. What will I say to her when my turn comes?

I should have known she'd be ready for me. The dying don't waste time when peace needs to be made. When we have a moment alone together, she looks right at me and says, "Honey, I'm sorry." I tell her if anyone ought to be sorry, it's me. I fight the part of me that wants to take this apology and tear it open, showing her everything that's inside it, every precise thing I'm sorry for and everything I want to hear her say she regrets. This slim peace is all we'll get, and I hold it in my mouth like hard candy, sucking it dry, trying to believe it's enough. But already I understand that I'm going to be talking to her long after she's gone. It isn't even over yet and the grief is already invading, like a fog that starts at the ankles and rises all the way up through the body.

I take a break from the bedside vigil and walk through my old town. It doesn't matter what's changed here; there's enough in the thickness of the air, the smell of the honeysuckle, to collapse the years in my mind. I see my mother coming home from work and me running to meet her, back when I wanted her purely, with everything I knew, when wanting wasn't laced with rage. Can I open myself to it again, every possible thing I feel for her? I cry as I walk, and think of Grady crying. Can I make my own vows? Can I offer myself that fully?

If I did, I'd have to say what I couldn't say that day in the jail: yes, Mom, I was capable of all that and more. I did things I can never take back. And I ran away from home so long ago, even when it looked like I was still here. There's a big hole in you where a son should be and I'll never fill that now; you'll never even know I'm trying. For years I hid myself from you and then cursed you for not seeing me. Don't you understand? I wanted you to see me anyway. Like a child playing the old game, I wanted you to come and find me where I hid.

When am I going to die, she asked, and of course we couldn't answer. But she must have felt it coming, because she dies later that day. Grady,

Joe, and I are with her. I hold her hand as she goes, and I think of all the times she said to me, "I could be dying and you wouldn't come home." I'm here, here enough to be crying, here enough to be sitting with her instead of running away. But I don't even know which one of us I'm crying for.

My grandmother's death, more than half my lifetime ago, left me stripped, desolate, resigned to being purely bad. What will this death leave me with? There are losses no one can restore. She didn't protect me, I didn't protect her. When she wrote to me in prison, she would tell me about young men in town who looked like me and made her think of what I could have been. Everywhere she looked, she couldn't help seeing what she didn't have. If I dare to look, I can't help seeing what I don't have either. But at the funeral, I stand up and talk about my mother, and I look out at all the people I haven't seen in years. I thought I had to come back a hero, but maybe it's enough just to have come back at all. I hear Bobby's voice saying, "Use your memories, don't let them use you." There's a way to live that isn't all about running. "*You* decide what you're going to become," Bobby told me fiercely, insisting that I see it. There's a road out of this town that's different from the road I took at 15, and I say to him, I say to her: that's the road I'm on.

I heard a story one time about a thief who robbed houses in his neighborhood. He was a boy, barely a man, and when he got caught the judge made it a condition of his sentence that he meet with the people he had robbed and work out some form of restitution. He sat down with a couple whose furniture he'd taken. Before they even started to talk about how he could repay them, the woman wanted to explain exactly how she and her husband had acquired the furniture and what each piece had meant to them. "I want you to understand what you took from us," she said.

What is taken is always more than anyone can imagine at the time. The theft, whether of furniture or innocence or trust, is always greater. *What you took*, I could say to the man who drove me to the side of a quiet road one night, and would he be as surprised as that furniture thief to hear how great the robbery, how lasting the damage? *What you took*, I could say to him and to so many others. And then could I sit and listen while people explained my own thieving to me? Declaring all the losses takes a long time. It's easier, sometimes, not to understand what was taken.

I say "what was taken," I use the passive voice, because sometimes it's too overwhelming to think about who did what. But I don't mean to blur the distinctions, so I'll say it this way: it would be easier not to understand what I took from people. It would be easier not to understand what people I trusted took from me. But I have seen how essential that understanding is. There is no going forward without it.

Of course, understanding alone can't restore what is lost. And even when there is some restoration, nothing comes back in exactly the same form. At best, what you get is replacement, like the table the thief searched for and managed to find, once he'd come to know the couple well enough to know what they would appreciate and value. They say now that when visiting friends set their coffee down on this new table, they compliment it and the hosts reply, "There's quite a story about this table." Sure enough, there is. It's the story of their ability to explain what was taken. It's the story of the boy's ability to see what he had done.

I like to think that when these people look at their table now, they don't think it means their loss didn't matter. Instead, maybe, what it means is that there is at least *something* solid that can be reclaimed, and offered.

What is taken is gone. There is no getting around that. That boy knew it, and I know it too. I hope with all these words to have made something solid that can, at least, be reclaimed, and offered.

Acknowledgments

In a Dark Time owes an enormous debt to Amanda Bergson-Shilcock, Meredith Collins, Lorraine and Joanna Hoyt, and Natalie Rusk, each of whom contributed a unique perspective as they wrote detailed comments on drafts of the manuscript. And week by week, Jeri Bayer and Suzanne Berger critiqued every line with a care and thoughtfulness that sets the standard for any writer's workshop.

Conversations with the following people were important during the years of work on the project: Jamie Bissonnette, Jill Brotman, Gene and Sue Burkart (at whose welcoming dinner table the whole thing began), Peggy Chace, Carolyn Coman, Anna Coman-Hidy, Renny Cushing, Marie Deans, Bobby Dellelo, Aaron Falbel, Lloyd Fillion, Michael Forcier, Andrew Huckins, Neal Katz, Suzanne MacDonald, Sarabeth Matilsky, Sean McGrath, Tom Rusk, Steve Saloom, the late Theo Seghorn, Taylor Stoehr, Rebecca Young. Each of these people were willing to consider hard questions about prison, criminal behavior, and the complexities of human growth and development, and their thoughts have had a powerful effect on the book. As well, the writings of James Gilligan, Alice Miller, David Cayley, and Jerome Miller have been influential.

A few of these individuals need to be mentioned a second time because of the myriad ways they have been part of the journey. They know how they have helped, what a difference they have made, and the ways in which they exemplify friendship and support at its best. Deepest gratitude to Natalie Rusk, Amanda Bergson-Shilcock, Jeri Bayer, Renny Cushing, Bobby Dellelo, and of course, for so many reasons, Aaron Falbel.

Thanks also to Pat Farenga, Angela Mark, and Grace Llewellyn for their skills in helping to turn the manuscript into a book, and to Bruegger's Porter Square and the 1369 Coffee House for unknowingly providing such hospitable space in which to carry out the work.

— Susannah Sheffer

About the Authors

Born in North Carolina, Dwight Harrison spent almost 17 years in Massachusetts prisons. He has spoken about his experiences to groups of lawmakers, university students, and other audiences.

Susannah Sheffer's previous books include *A Life Worth Living* and *A Sense of Self,* and her essays and poems have appeared in numerous magazines and journals. She writes frequently about both prison issues and victims' issues.